The Scandalous God

The
Scandalous God

The Use and Abuse of the Cross

Vítor Westhelle

Fortress Press
Minneapolis

THE SCANDALOUS GOD
The Use and Abuse of the Cross

"The Emperor Contantine" by Czeslaw Milosz, tr. Czeslaw Milosz and Robert Haas, from *Second Space: New Poems*, © 2004 by Czeslaw Milosz. All rights reserved. Reprinted by permission of HarperCollins.
"Luke XXIII", translated by Mark Strand, copyright © 1999 by Maria Kodama, translation copyright © 1999 by Mark Strand, from *Selected Poems* by Jorge Luis Borges, edited by Alexander Coleman. Used by permission of Viking Penguin, a division of Penguin Group (USA) Inc.
Pier Paolo Pasolini, poem from Michael Hardt, "Exposure: Pasolini in the Flesh," in Brian Mannumi, ed., *A Shock to Thought: Expression after Deleuze and Guattari* (London: Routledge, 2002). Used by permission.
Excerpt from "The Way of Pain" from *Collected Poems: 1957-1982* by Wendell Berry. Copyright © 1985 by Wendell Berry. Reprinted by permission of North Point Press, a division of Farrar, Straus and Girooux. LLC.
Scripture quotations are from the New Revised Standard Version Bible, © 1989 by the Division of Christian Education of the National Council of the Churches of Christ in the USA. Used by permission. All rights reserved.

Cover image: *Crucifixion*, Graham Sutherland © Estate of Graham Sutherland. Used by permission
Cover design: Abby Hartman

Library of Congress Cataloging-in-Publication Data
Westhelle, Vítor, 1952-
The scandalous God : the use and abuse of the cross / Vítor Westhelle.
    p. cm.
ISBN-13: 978-0-8006-3895-5 (alk. paper)
ISBN-10: 0-8006-3895-6 (alk. paper)
    1. Jesus Christ—Crucifixion—History of doctrines. 2. Jesus Christ—Crucifixion. I. Title.
BT453.W47 2007
232'.4—dc22
                                2006025386

The paper used in this publication meets the minimum requirements of American National Standard for Information Sciences—Permanence of Paper for Printed Library Materials, ANSI Z329.48-1984.
Manufactured in the U.S.A.

11   10   09   08   07   2   3   4   5   6   7   8   9   10

Contents

Chapter 6
Cross and Poetry
The Mask of God and Human Accountability toward Creation
93

Chapter 7
The Practice of Resurrection
On Asserting the Openness of Past Victimizations
108

Chapter 8
A "Theory" of the Cross
The Human Arts: *Poiesis, Praxis,* and *Theoria*
125

Chapter 9
Cross and Eschatology
The Ends of the World
144

Chapter 10
The Stations of the Cross Revisited
Via Crucis et Resurrectionis
160

Preface

"**A theologian of the cross** calls the thing what it actually is," wrote Martin Luther in one of his famous theses for the Heidelberg Disputation. The intention of this work is to present the cross of Christ for what it actually is. This work is also about naming a scandal, a stumbling block that is at the heart of Christianity. The word *scandal* also has the meaning of "offense." With the cross God becomes offensive. While this may seem a provocative statement, it is a plain rendition of 2 Corinthians 5:21: Christ was "made to be sin who knew no sin." In the New Testament sin is exegetically defined as "missing the mark." One can miss the mark either by making a mistake with the target or by failing to reach it. In either case the missing of the mark, which we call sin, creates lacunae in our lives. As the pieces of a jigsaw puzzle when fitted into the gaps give a true sense of the picture, the scandal or the stumbling block of the cross fills the lacunae in our lives, thereby rendering meaning to the meaninglessness, putting us in touch with the reality that surrounds us.

But even the utterance of the cross as a scandal is a gamble, for it leads to the possibility of domesticating what I am naming or rendering it into a concept that can be constrained properly. Thorns of history are often sublimated and administered by intellectual systems. In what follows I run the risk of saying too much because the scandal concerns the life and death of God then and now, in all of God's creation. The theology of the cross is neither a discourse nor a doctrine. It is a way of life that we live out. It is a practice that involves a risk. It is a story that, if truly told, courts danger but moves also into hopeful solidarity, the solidarity of those who are moved by the pain of God in the midst of this world, or by the pain of the world in the midst of God.

This book has two foci. The first is historical and traces the development of the cross motif throughout the history of the church, sketching its source of inspiration and its simultaneous recurrent domestication. Chapters 1 through 4 take on that task. The second focus is primarily thematic and deals with the theological intricacies of a theme that has been at the same time fascinating but also criticized and evaded theologically and philosophically. Chapters 5 through 10 explore that theology for today. It eventually begs the question, What difference would it have made if Jesus had just died of old age and not on the cross? And if the cross does make a difference, what does it ask of us today?

Can we read the signs? How much does it take for us to see what the cross asks of us? Do we read the signs of the sun darkening? Do we see the exiled, the abandoned, the aged, and impoverished and still not know that every poor person impoverishes us even as we dwell in luxury and that each one that is uprooted takes away from us some of our own grounding? Do we see the children on the streets, the women abused in the silence of their homes? Do we see those left homeless? Don't we know that every homeless person makes the places in which we live a little less than a home? Do we read the message in the moon losing its light? And the falling stars, do we see them? Are we really aware that any loss, anyone that has been taken away from us for any reason or is being kept from our embrace, diminishes us, even if we are not quite dead yet? What will it take for us to see the cross in our midst and call it for what it is? Yes, naming a thing for what it actually is, is indeed risky, but it also is a promise. And that is the story of the cross in which you and I live.

In simple terms, this story of scandal and promise is like the Shabbat, the day God takes a break, does nothing, when we are given the holy right to pray and play. But this Shabbat is also the day we mourn the death of God, God in all of creation that God has assumed in order to redeem, as we have been instructed since the early church. We live in this pendular movement, which swings between two realities that God died and God lives. This is the story of you and me. But we so often evade the scandal, embellish life to hide the pain, deny death and the cross that is in and around us, and thus often miss what follows, the Sunday of resurrection.

This is then the impasse with which I am faced. My intent is to evoke the scandal, the shame of exposure, the danger of a memory that never ought to be edited down or beautified. For the evocation I need language, however, an organized and hopefully elegant ensemble of symbols to convey that which defies organization and closure. Symbols elicit thinking; they give rise to thought, as we have been taught. They help us to think about our reality, our condition, by pointing to another reality, thus giving us a sense, a foretaste of it. If in evoking here the scandal through these symbols and words I elicit thoughts about the pain and death, the crosses in and around us, I will have accomplished what I set out to do. To this end I offer this work so that we might rejoice when Sunday comes.

This book has been in the works for years. People I have met, places I have visited, and memories I have collected along the way have been my companions in this endeavor and were my conversation partners as I penned the various chapters. Earlier versions of two of the chapters, "The Practice of Resurrection" and "Cross and Eschatology," have appeared in *Seminary Ridge Review* 8/2 (Spring 2006), 31–43 and in *Currents in Theology and Mission* 27/2: 85–97, respectively. I am grateful to both publications. Numerous courses on the subject, with remarkable students from many parts of the world whose quizzical minds not only prodded me on but also stimulated my musings, added much richness to this project. They also made me realize what a daunting task it is to write on a topic such as this. To my students, of yore and now, I offer my homage. My colleagues over the years have been wonderful in their support, as have the administrations of the places I taught at for the last quarter of a century, particularly in recent years the Lutheran School of Theology at Chicago.

Calling upon names is always a risk, because the one left out might have been particularly significant. But then, this is a book about the cross, about failure, about God being a failure. The debt one has accumulated in heart and mind, in time and space will never be paid; this is the insurmountable betrayal. And we can assert this honestly only by adding that it will be collected and all will be forgiven and nothing will be forgotten, for no gesture of love will ever be lost.

But there are some people that have been direct accomplices in the weaving of this manuscript for what they have taught me. Hermann Brandt, Walter Altmann, Juan Luis Segundo, José Míguez-Bonino, my Ph.D. advisor and later colleague Philip Hefner, Oswald Bayer, Viggo Mortensen, José David Rodriguez, Kadi Billman, Reinhard Hütter, Cynthia Jürissson, Barbara Rossing, Richard Jensen, David Rhoads, Antje Jackelén, Kurt Hendel, Harold Vogelaar, Audrey West, Albert (Pete) Pero, and Mark Thomsen (with whom I taught "Theology of the Cross")—to all of you who have inspired and informed this book, I owe my sincere gratitude.

For someone who is barely fluent in his own mother tongue, Portuguese, the work of editors is indispensable while writing in another language and making a text coherent. Michael West at Fortress Press has been that editor who gave the much-needed support for this publication along with the helpful staff at Augsburg Fortress. A word of recognition and thanks to Ronald Bonner, who introduced the manuscript to Fortress Press. Sandra Roberts and David Rhoads worked countless hours on the grammar and style providing sharp but helpful criticisms and comments, thus enhancing the script's leaps and bounds. Ann Hafften and David Lott did the final editorial work, setting the text in order and simplifying a tortured and convoluted English. But none of this would have been accomplished without the help of Mary (Joy) Philip, a former professor of biology, my assistant and doctoral candidate in Theology. She has been nothing but a joy in this painstaking process. Thank you, my friends.

My final and immense debt and gratitude goes to my family, Christiane, Janelle, Carlos, André, and Felipe, for their love and support, with due apologies for the time this has taken me away from them.

Evasions of the Scandal

Religion decays, the icon remains; a narrative is forgotten, yet its representation still magnetizes.... Indeed, history democratizes our sympathies.

Julian Barnes

The questions the first Christians faced, when they experienced Jesus' crucifixion, were nothing if not extremely disturbing. Why did the Messiah die? Is there a meaning in meaninglessness? How could the One who worked healing die the "vilest death"?[1] Should some tragic juridical error, a regrettable mistake alone, a "misunderstanding" of his actions account for it, as some have suggested?[2] The shock that overtook the first disciples became embedded in Christian tradition as a valorous effort to circumvent this vile death and its importance in the discursive nexus of Christian theology. Later, the cross was an incongruent episode in the story of the God of love for the Christian Gnostics and Peter Abelard and remains so in modern times with Friedrich Schleiermacher and his descendants, in some feminist and in so-called liberal theologies.

---

[1] The expression is from Origen; see Martin Hengel, *Crucifixion in the Ancient World and the Folly of the Message of the Cross* (Philadelphia: Fortress Press, 1977), xi.

[2] In modern theology this position was strongly sustained by Rudolf Bultmann, *Die Verhältnis der urchristliche Christusbotschaft zum historischen Jesus* (Heidelberg: Carl Winter, 1962), 12.

And for good reason: the cross either offends rationality or becomes a tool to perpetuate an anemic will and a slave-like disposition.

From a crude reality, the cross gradually became a symbol to identify the Christian faith. There is no harmony between the reality and the ensuing symbol, however. The symbol often swallows the historical scandal that gave it birth and appeases the appalling experience with which the first generations of Christians had to come to terms. Faced with mockery from opponents, they stood firm in their sustaining that which the world regarded as foolish. Indeed, the enemies of Christianity, according to New Testament scholar Walter Bauer, "always referred to the disgracefulness of the death of Jesus with great emphasis and malicious pleasure. A god or son of god dying on the cross! That was enough to put paid to the new religion."[3] And yet it was their unabashed boldness in affirming that shameful scandal—claiming as Lord a convicted and executed criminal, proclaiming the word of the cross—that anchored the centrality and novelty of the "new"[4] religion, or what Friedrich Nietzsche once called "Christianity's stroke of genius: God offering himself for the guilt of humans."[5] Indeed, it is amazing that a religion was founded on the experience of utter shame, of a god that dies the death of a condemned criminal.

A century and a half after the crucifixion, the cross of Jesus was still a source of wonder and bewilderment and yet kept its sharp paradoxical character. The words of Melito of Sardis, a second-century martyr, testify to the scandal:

> He that hung up the earth *in space* was *Himself* hanged up; He that fixed the heavens was fixed *with nails*; He that bore up the earth was borne up on a tree; the Lord *of all* was subject to ignomy in a naked body—God put to death! The King of Israel slain with Israel's right hand! Alas for the new wickedness of the new murder! The Lord was exposed with naked

---

[3] See Hengel, *Crucifixion in the Ancient World*, 19.

[4] The term *new* can only be used in hindsight, for the first Christians still understood themselves as a messianic movement within Judaism.

[5] Friedrich Nietzsche, *Werke in zwei Bänden* (Leipzig: Alfred Kröner, 1930), 2:123.

body: He was not deemed worthy even of covering; and, in order that He might not be seen, the luminaries turned away, and the day became darkened, because they slew God, who hung naked on the tree.[6]

Two millennia after the event, we are a long way from those historical circumstances to grasp fully the boldness of early Christians' affirming that the One on the cross was truly God *and* human, a formulation that came to be stated with such succinct bluntness only four centuries later, although mainstream Christians read it out of the pages of the New Testament and found it foretold already in the Hebrew Scriptures. As we shall see, temptations to give up such radical oddity were many from early on. Early Ebionism, later revised in the very popular Arian compromise, claimed for Jesus less than full divinity, thus dissolving or at least softening the paradox of the divine suffering, of the infinite reduced to finitude, of the glorious One found in utter shame, the Almighty facing total weakness. The other option was the sophisticated Docetist solutions, backed by robust Gnostic philosophical systems, denying the full humanity and therefore the suffering of the Christ. But none of these tempting solutions were finally adopted in mainstream or "orthodox" Christianity.

Options for Evading the Cross

To this day the problems the cross presents are still raised, many by recycling early options for evading the scandal and the folly. In a poem written by António Machado in the 1920s, this uneasiness with the cross is well expressed. He writes in response to a *saeta*—a popular Spanish song chanted in religious processions—that went like this:

> Who will lend me a ladder
> to get up the cross
> and remove the nails
> of Jesus, the Nazarene?

---

[6] *Ante-Nicene Fathers* (Peabody, Mass.: Hendrickson, 1994), 8:757b.

Machado's retort to the *saeta* was a call to abandon the popular obsession with the passionalism of his Iberian culture, the sublimation of pain into piety:

> Oh, this song that sings
> to the Christ of the Gypsies
> always with blood in his hands
> always waiting to be released!
> Song from the people of Andalusia
> who, in every Spring,
> go out asking for ladders
> to climb up the cross!
> Song of my land
> that throws flowers
> to the Jesus of agony
> and is the faith of my elders!
> Oh, that is not my song!
> I don't want and will not sing
> to this Jesus of the tree,
> but to the one who walked on the sea![7]

Such criticism of the use and abuse of the cross foreshadows many contemporary critics who see the role played by the cross in theology as a justification or sublimation of violence and abuse, as often happens in many atonement theories and models.[8]

---

[7] "¡Oh, la saeta, el cantar/al Cristo de los gitanos,/siempre con sangre en las manos, siempre pro desenclavar!/¡Cantar del pueblo andaluz,/que todas las primaveras/anda pidiendo escaleras/para subir a la cruz!/¡Cantar de la tierra mía,/que echa flores/al Jesús de la agonía,/y es la fe de mis mayores!/¡Oh, no eres tu mi cantar!/¡No uedo cantar, ni quiero/a ese Jesús del madero,/sino al que anduvo en el mar!" Antonio Machado, *Poesías* (Buenos Aires: Losada, 1977), 149–50.

[8] Examples of such criticism of atonement theories can be found in *Christianity, Patriarchy, and Abuse*, ed. Joanne C. Brown and Carole Bohn (Cleveland: Pilgrim Press, 1989) in several of its chapters. Also see Gerhard Forde, *A More Radical Gospel* (Grand Rapids: Eerdmans, 2004), 101–13; Sally Purvis, *The Power of the Cross* (Nashville: Abingdon Press, 1993). From an African American perspective see Johnny R. Youngblood, "Growing in the Power of the 'Resurrected' Christ," *Punctuations* (April 16, 1995), 5–11.

The crucifixion is an historical event that defies comprehension and eludes meaning. Struggling with such events, which G. W. F. Hegel once conceded were "the thorns of history," can achieve some sense in two ways: either by weakening some of the claims attributed to these events and strengthening others or by evoking a novel cause not previously taken into account. Such was the case with the crucifixion.

In the case of Jesus' life, crucifixion, and resurrection, Ebionism and Docetism early on brought some logic into a messy set of paradoxes by either weakening or strengthening claims about Jesus' humanity and his divinity. Ebionism and its successors (Adoptionism and several variants of Arianism) downplayed the divinity of Jesus so the radical transcendence of God would not be compromised—God just could not die the death of a convicted criminal. Docetism and its descendants within various Gnostic-inspired circles did the opposite and minimized the claim of Jesus' humanity—they spared God the frailty and humiliation of actual flesh. For the early Christian Docetists, the cross was only the appearance (*dokein*) of a brutal experience. "The son of God had only *seemed* to be crucified. In reality he did not suffer at all."[9]

Some Gnostic writers found a novel cause: they fancied that someone else was crucified in Jesus' place. With the Enlightenment the argument for the "apparent" death of Jesus was often proposed, alongside a version of the novel-cause suggestion that Jesus, in the absence of reliable evidence, was not even a historical person.

The poignancy of such criticisms continues to produce results, leading many to abandon the cross or call for its "abolition."[10] It is judged and deemed to be irredeemable in Christian theology. Instead of the cross, two other christological foci are lifted up to prevent the abuse: one moves from the cross to the life and teachings of Jesus, the other to the resurrection. The first argument insists that it is the life of Jesus as a source of renewal for Christian life and thought that should be affirmed. The second moves in the opposite direction, finding in the resurrection narratives a source of empowerment and life.

---

[9] Hengel, *Crucifixion in the Ancient World*, 21.

[10] Choan Seng Song, "Christian Mission toward the Abolition of the Cross," in *The Scandal of a Crucified World*, ed. Yacob Tesfai (Maryknoll, N.Y.: Orbis Books, 1994), 130–48.

J. Louis Martyn, in his study of Paul's letters to the Corinthians, found such options of evading the cross already represented in early Christianity, offering ways of avoiding the theological problems of extracting meaning from the event of the cross. This avoidance is only accomplished, however, by retreating from the cross in favor of the life of Jesus or superseding it with the resurrection. "The essential failure of the Corinthians," writes Martyn, "consists in their inflexible determination to live either *before* the cross (the super-apostles of 2 Corinthians) or *after* the cross (the Gnostics of 1 Corinthians) rather than *in* the cross."[11]

From the Ebionites[12] of the first century through the Arians to some modern liberal theology, the first option conveyed the idea that the crucifixion, real and scandalous as it was, marked the tragic end of a man. It signaled, at most, the final fate of the One who was faithful to the end and pointed back to his life of faithfulness to God's calling. The cross becomes a hermeneutical key to interpret Jesus' life. The resurrection is framed as a narrative to indicate in fantastic imagery that God has vindicated that loss and affirmed that life. Here we have a theology *before* the cross.

In our day this is an attractive solution, as feminist theologian Julie Hopkins attests:

> The divinization of Jesus by the Church Fathers does not explain what happened on the cross; it only confuses the issue. If the Greco-Roman world was scandalized by the Christian message of the vulnerable God it only made the problem more intractable if one argued that Jesus was also in part divine.[13]

[11] J. Louis Martyn, "Epistemology at the Turn of the Ages: 2 Corinthians 5:16," in *Christian History and Interpretation: Studies Presented to John Knox*, ed. W. R. Farmer, C. F. D. Moule, and R. R. Niebuhr (Cambridge: Cambridge University Press, 1967), 285.

[12] Ebionites formed an early Jewish-Christian sect that was so named after the self-description of early followers of Jesus as "the poor ones," *ebion* in Hebrew. See H. J. Schoepps, "Die ebionitische Warheit des Christentums," in *The Background of the New Testament and its Eschatology*, ed. W. D. Davies and D. Daube (Cambridge: Cambridge University Press, 1956), 115–23.

[13] Julie M. Hopkins, *Towards a Feminist Christology: Jesus of Nazareth, European Women, and the Christological Crisis* (Grand Rapids: Eerdmans, 1994), 58. Making the case for the "intractable" role of the cross, New Testament scholar Roy A. Harrisville, in *Fracture: The Cross as Irreconcilable in the Language and Thought of the Biblical Writers* (Grand Rapids: Eerdmans, 2006), argues that for the New Testament authors, "despite attempts at eliminating its turbulence, the cross denotes an activity that defies repression, perhaps even expression…a thing beyond telling, out of the reach of words."

Yet what is decisive is that Jesus was not claimed to be "partly divine" but indeed wholly so: *vere Deus*.

The other option, represented by early Christian Docetism and Gnosticism, finds its post-Enlightenment adherents in several relevant traditions in theology. It emphasizes the resurrection as affirmation of the strength of life, dismissing or weakening the implications of the scandal of the cross. In modern times the point is not so much a denial of Jesus' full humanity but a view of the cross as a counterpoint that magnifies the resurrection. Given that the cross is an unavoidable part of the Christian narrative, it can only be framed and read from the standpoint of the resurrection: "On Good Friday the resurrected one was crucified."[14]

Schleiermacher, the so-called father of modern theology, saw that humans are able to overcome some suffering by discipline and piety. He claimed that "our own experience teaches us that an ordinary ethical development and robust piety have as their reward the almost complete overcoming of physical suffering in the presence of a glad spiritual self-consciousness."[15] If we mere humans can "almost completely" surmount suffering, then the one with perfect God-consciousness could do so perfectly. The cross itself is not the traumatic event it seems and does not need to be, for Christ's "sufferings themselves have the loosest connexion with His reaction against sin."[16] This stance flirts with the Gnostic denial of suffering. Following Martyn's terminology, this can be called a theology *after* the cross.

These options soften some of the paradoxes associated with the crucifixion. Understanding the real brutality of crucifixion may bring us an important dose of reality, however. There is something inescapable about the role of the cross in Christian theology, an unresolved riddle that keeps surfacing. As Martin Hengel pointed out in his study of the crucifixion practice in antiquity,

---

[14] Joanne C. Brown and Rebecca Parker, "For God So Loved the World?" in *Christianity, Patriarchalism, and Abuse*, 28.

[15] Friedrich Schleiermacher, *The Christian Faith* (Edinburgh: T & T Clark, 1989), 437.

[16] Ibid.

The particular form of the death of Jesus, the man and the messiah, represents a scandal which people would like to blunt, remove or domesticate in any way possible. We shall have to guarantee the truth of our theological thinking at this point. Reflection on the harsh reality of crucifixion in antiquity may help us to overcome the acute loss of reality which is to be found so often in present theology and preaching.[17]

The Symbol: Emergence and Sublimation[18]

We have discussed strategies for bringing the cross event into some logical coherence by evading its more radical—and indeed paradoxical—claims. Another way to deal with "thorns of history" is to sublimate them and domesticate their meaning, removing them from their original historical context. Following the suggestion of novelist Julian Barnes, this process can be aptly, yet ironically, described as a "democratization of our sympathies." How does this work?

Susan Sontag's last book about photography, *Regarding the Pain of Others*, points to the process of symbolic domestication and sublimation. While photography has a unique claim to the faithful depiction of reality, a process of sublimation can be observed. She writes:

There is beauty in ruins. To acknowledge the beauty of photographs of the World Trade Center ruins in the months following the attacks seemed frivolous, sacrilegious. The most people dared say was that the photographs were "surreal," a hectic euphemism behind which the disgraced notion of beauty cowered. But they *were* beautiful, many of them....The site itself, the mass graveyard that received the name "Ground Zero," was of course anything but beautiful. Photographs tend to transform, whatever their subject; and as an image something may be beautiful—or terrifying, or unbearable, or quite bearable—as it is not in real life.[19]

---

[17] Hengel, *Crucifixion in the Ancient World*, 90.

[18] *Symbol* will be used here not in Paul Tillich's technical sense ("A symbol participates in the reality it symbolizes," *Systematic Theology*, 3 vols. [Chicago: University of Chicago Press, 1951–1963], 1:177), but in its common acceptations as a figurative representation.

[19] Susan Sontag, *Regarding the Pain of Others* (New York: Farrar, Straus & Giroux, 2003), 76.

Sontag summarizes her point by saying, "The problem is not that people remember through photographs, but that they remember only the photographs. This remembering through photographs eclipses other forms of understanding, and remembering."[20] If even photographs, this modern invention to portray reality "as it is," can replace the actuality of an event for its representation, arts that have less a claim on actuality itself—such as movies, paintings, emblems, drawings, and so forth—are even more likely to displace that which is portrayed by the portrayal itself.

When Mel Gibson's movie *The Passion of the Christ* was previewed at the Vatican, the press reported that Pope John Paul II said, "This is exactly how it happened." While the Vatican never confirmed that statement, it is an anecdotal example of this displacement. A movie that, unlike a photograph, was not filmed at the scene, goes beyond displacement to constructing a historical event "exactly how it happened." Needless to say, the movie does it beautifully, artfully, in spite of *and* because of the pain and violence it portrays. Sontag, whose book antedates the movie, observes the connection of this process with religion. Such "a view of suffering, of the pain of others is rooted in religious thinking, which links pain to sacrifice, sacrifice to exaltation."[21]

This vicarious displacement of the actual affects figurative representations, simulacra, symbols, and emblems. By the Constantinian era (but, not before[22]) the symbol of the cross had gained broad acceptance as the major figurative representation of the Christian faith, starting in the time of Theodosius I in the fourth quarter of the fourth century.[23] The shocking reality of the cross was often concealed behind the plethora of its use. The cross of defeat, and *in it* the daring affirmation of triumph in the appearance of shame and foolishness, became the cross of the triumph of Constantine and later of the Crusades and the conquest of the New World. *Behind* it was an often forgotten and artfully veiled historical scandal.

---

[20] Ibid., 89.

[21] Ibid., 99.

[22] See Erich Dinkler, *Signum Crucis: Aufsätze zum Neuen Testament und zur Christliche Archäologie* (Tübingen: J. C. B. Mohr [Paul Siebeck], 1967), 72–73.

[23] Ibid., 73.

The era of mechanical and later electronic reproduction hastened the process that keeps the event behind and substitutes by a representation.[24] Erich Dinkler, in his study of the cross as a symbolic representation in early Christianity, has insisted on the effects resulting from an excess of employment of the symbol.

> We are today…so accustomed to the symbol of the cross—be it as a symbol of Christianity, or as a symbol of secular humanism as in the Red Cross or the Blue Cross or even as a political emblem—that the scandalous in it, and the scandal itself, no longer seem to strike us.[25]

In fact, Dinkler goes on, "the adoption of the cross of Christ as symbol was made possible precisely over the notions of *triumph*.…Yes, it became sublimated and thus the cross was…introduced into art."[26] Certainly from early layers of New Testament material to the writings of Irenaeus there were attempts to indicate a victory *hidden in* defeat. The development of the use of the cross as representative of Constantinian Christianity turned it into a symbol of victory *over* the defeated, however.

The emblematic motto of Constantine, inscribed with the cross on the shields of his army before the king's battle against Maxientius's army in 312, is revealing: *in hoc signo vinces*, "by this sign you win." This maxim was unfurled again and again in the Crusades, which literally describes an enterprise "of the cross," and in all Christian triumphalism to this day.

Spirituality: The Scandal Underneath

Even in sublimation and glorification, the cross retains a submerged potential for rocking the boat of theological hegemony. It does so in spite of the cry of triumph that deafens the scandal. Polish poet Czeslaw

---

[24] See the pertinent observations regarding this phenomenon in Walter Benjamin, "The Work of Art in the Age of Mechanical Reproduction, in *Illuminations* (New York: Schocken, 1968), 217–51.

[25] Dinkler, *Signum Crucis*, 71.

[26] Ibid., 73.

Milosz phrased this with surprising sharpness, using as an example who else but Constantine:

> I could have lived in the time of Constantine.
> Three hundred years after the death of the Savior,
> Of whom no more was known than that he had risen
> Like a sunny Mithra among Roman legionnaires.
> I would have witnessed the quarrel between *homoousios* and *homoiousios*
> About whether the Christ nature is divine or only resembles divinity.
> Probably I would have cast my vote against Trinitarians,
> For who could ever guess the Creator's nature?
> Constantine, Emperor of the World, coxcomb and murderer,
> Tipped the scale at the Council of Nicea,
> So that we, generation after generation, meditate on the Holy Trinity,
> Mystery of mysteries, without which
> The blood of man would have been alien to the blood of the universe
> And the spilling of His own blood by a suffering God,
> who offered Himself
> As a sacrifice even as He was creating the world, would have been in vain.
> Thus Constantine was merely an undeserving tool,
> Unaware of what he was doing for people of distant times?
> And us, do we know what we are destined for?[27]

Martin Luther was one who knew what he was destined for. Studying the theology of the cross, he discovered this process the symbol went through—of displacement from actuality to representation. The Reformer found in the profusion of the use of the cross the dissolution of its disturbing uneasiness. Yet the discomforting sharpness of the cross could not be erased either by evasion or sublimation, or by Constantine's heritage of triumphalism (the emperor "was merely an undeserving tool, unaware of what he was doing").

---

[27] Czelaw Milosz, "The Emperor Constantine," translated from the Polish by the author and Robert Hass, *New York Review of Books* 51, no. 14 (September 23, 2004): 65.

In "A Meditation on Christ's Passion," from 1519, Luther reflects about the use and abuse of the symbol of the cross in popular and theological piety. Not unlike Susan Sontag, he concludes with contempt: "We have transformed the essence into semblance and painted our meditations on Christ's passion on walls and made them into letters."[28] In the Ninety-Five Theses (more celebrated than read), written in 1517, a year earlier than the famous statements about the theology of the cross in the Heidelberg Disputation, we find these two theses:

> 92. Away then with all those prophets who say to the people of Christ, "Peace, peace" and there is no peace (Jer 6:14).
> 93. Blessed be all those prophets who say to the people of Christ "Cross, cross," and there is no cross.[29]

The symmetry between the two theses is conspicuous. As much as the appearance of a peaceful empire disguised the lack of peace in the social strife at Luther's time, the abundance of crosses mitigated the shocking reality the cross should represent for life and theology.[30] The overabundance of the symbol turned it into an idol, which, as idols do, displaced the gaze of the beholder from its literal and actual meaning to the representation itself.

We are faced with a classical hermeneutical problem: How are we to translate meaning while not betraying intent; how are we to translate without traducing (the two share the same etymological root)? Since patristic times it has been customary to distinguish between the literal or historical sense and the spiritual or allegorical sense in interpreting the Scriptures. The latter is further divided into three different types: the allegorical proper or typological, the moral or tropological, and the eschatological or anagogical meaning.

---

[28] Martin Luther, "A Meditation on Christ's Passion," *Luther's Works* vol. 42, *Devotional Writings I*, vol. ed. Martin O. Dietrich, trans. Martin Bertram (Philadelphia: Fortress Press, 1969), 14.

[29] Martin Luther, "Heidelberg Disputation (1518)," *Luther's Works* vol. 33, *Career of the Reformer I*, ed. and trans. Harold J. Grimm (Philadelphia: Fortress Press, 1957), 33.

[30] See Philip Ruge-Jones, "Cross in Tensions: Theology of the Cross as Theologico-Social Critique," unpublished Ph.D. dissertation (Lutheran School of Theology, 1999).

In Scholasticism the four senses were called the *quadriga*. Thomas Aquinas offers the classic definition of them:

> That first meaning whereby the words signify things belongs to the sense first-mentioned, namely the historical or literal. That meaning, however, whereby the things by the words in their turn also signify other things is called the spiritual sense; it is based on and presupposes the literal sense. Now this spiritual sense is divided into three. For, as St Paul says, *the Old Law is the figure of the New*, and the New Law itself, as Dionysius says, is *the figure of the glory to come*. Then again, under the New Law the deeds wrought by our Head are signs also of what we ourselves ought to do. Well then, the allegorical sense is brought into play when the things of the Old Law signify the things of the New Law; the moral sense when the things done in Christ and those who prefigured him are signs of what we should carry out; and the anagogical sense when the things that lie ahead in eternal glory are signified.[31]

In the *quadriga* the senses were conceived as complementary. Their objective was to take out of a text or a word the broadest spectrum of meaning possible without falling into contradiction. However, the spiritual sense was frequently applied to literal texts and words that seemed too mundane and did not carry an edifying message—edifying as judged by the commentator. In his treatise "On the Catechising of the Uninstructed," Augustine skillfully reveals the impasse and implication with the problem of interpretation:

> Next we should take occasion by that ceremony to admonish him that, if he hears anything even in the Scriptures which may carry a carnal sound, he should, even although he fails to understand it, nevertheless believe that something spiritual is signified thereby, which bears upon holiness of character and the future life.[32]

---

[31] In Tzvetan Todorov, *Symbolism and Interpretation* (Ithaca: Cornell University Press, 1982), 112–13.

[32] "On the Catechising of the Uninstructed" (xxvi, 50), in *Nicene and Post-Nicene Fathers* (Peabody, Mass.: Hendickson, 1995), 3:312.

Even if the correct interpretation is missed, the intention is redeeming:

> If...a man draws a meaning from them [Holy Scriptures] that may be used for the building up of love, even though he does not happen upon the precise meaning which the author whom he reads intended to express in that place, his error is not pernicious, and he is wholly clear from the charge of deception.[33]

For Augustine, it is clear that the criterion guiding the range of possible spiritual interpretations lies in the twofold commandment, the love of God and of the neighbor. He combines allegory with what later was regarded to be the tropological or moral sense and the anagogical or eschatological sense. Yet the problem with such interpretative technique can be well exemplified with the message of the cross, where it is precisely the love criterion that is the question and not the answer, not the spiritual telos (goal), toward which the message points. Only a draconian effort can take the earliest accounts of the event, with its finale decrying Jesus' forsakenness, and turn this into an allegory of love. In other words, one can say that a narrative like the Exodus, a parable, or a miracle might be plausibly interpreted as pointing to the fulfillment of the love commandment. All these examples can easily be ruled by the criterion of "the building up of love," but not so with the crucifixion accounts as they come to us in the earlier layers of the tradition.

The story of the crucifixion and the cry of the forsaken One must be the disturbance of our understanding of the meaning of love. How can one say that the story of the crucifixion and the cry of the One who was forsaken is anything other than the disturbance of our own apprehension of what love means? In the cross the love criterion itself is shaken and we cannot retrieve it as long as the literal meaning stands.

The literal meaning of the *logos tou staurou* (word of the cross) shows itself to be irreducible to a spiritual (allegorical, tropological, or anagogical) interpretation in which it would receive a single, integral, final, and self-

---

[33] "On Christian Doctrine" (I, XXXVI, 40) in ibid., 2:533.

contained meaning. The *logos tou staurou* is an incision that cuts through any contiguity between the literal and spiritual meanings of the cross. It defies and rejects any attempt to settle on a spiritual meaning of the cross that displaces the literal and eases or resolves its disturbing tensions.

The particularity of the cross, its literal meaning and the attributes attached to the person of Jesus cannot be washed away with an allegorical soap. Its meaning is at once ultimate and yet fragmentary.[34] Ultimate, because it has the apocalyptic urgency of calling the event God's final revelation; fragmentary, not because it is a disjointed narrative, but because it fragments our attempt to hold it as an integral whole, administer and control it at our whim. This is what a scandal means; it disrupts an expected fulfillment and enclosure of meaning. The pursuance of the scandal is the agenda for the reflection that follows.

---

[34] This fragmentation of meaning that reaches its climax in the accounts of the crucifixion is also true for the biblical material as a whole. For the Old Testament, see Erhard Gerstenberger, *Theologies in the Old Testament* (Minneapolis: Fortress Press, 2002). For the New Testament, Ernst Käsemann, "Begründet der neutestamentliche Kanon die Einheit der Kirche?" in *Exegetische Versuche und Besinnungen*, 2 vols. (Göttingen: Vandenhoeck & Ruprecht, 1964), 1:214–23; and David Rhoads, *The Challenge of Diversity: The Witness of Paul and the Gospels* (Minneapolis: Fortress Press, 1996).

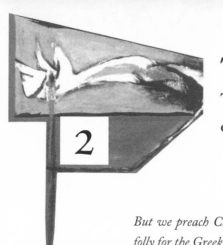

The Scandalous God

The Early Stages of a Theology of the Cross

2

But we preach Christ crucified: scandal for the Jews, folly for the Greeks..

1 Corinthians 1:23

Early Jewish-Christian Theological Frames

The early Christian development of a "theology"[1] of the cross took place largely within the context of Jewish piety as it unfolded during the intertestamental period and well into the second century of the Common Era. These "Jewish insights acquired down the centuries (independent of Jesus of Nazareth)," writes Edward Schillebeeckx, "are something [that] is impossible to dismiss. On the contrary, these already existing ideas helped the Jew, now become a Christian, to place in context and understand the life and destiny of the Master he already venerated and worshipped; they were not the cause of that veneration."[2] While these insights from Jewish piety were not the cause for reverence, they became the frame for the Christian Jew to cope with their experience of the life and fate of Jesus.

---

[1] That there is a "God-talk" (theology) in relation to the cross in the early Christian community is, as we shall see, an overstatement.

[2] Edward Schillebeeckx, *Jesus: An Experiment in Christology* (New York: Crossroad, 1981), 287–88.

This piety comes from sources and traditions of prayers of lament. While the voices of lament do not encompass all there is to the Jewish prayer and piety, the "voice of pain keeps prayer anchored in real life experience" assert Kathleen Billman and Daniel Migliore.[3] "Israel's faith and hope are all the more remarkable for refusing to stifle the voice of anger, pain and despair."[4] This tradition of lament calls for God's help in the midst of trial and distress yet does not attribute any redeeming meaning to suffering itself.

> Israel does not pretend to greater knowledge than it has. It can only cry that there are times when it experiences not God's justice, but injustice and undeserved suffering and thus the hiddenness of Yahweh's face....In this terrible hiddenness of God, Israel cries out, "How long, O God?" (Ps 13:1) "My God, my God, why have you forsaken me?" (Ps 22:1)[5]

The early search for meaning of the scandalous event of the one who was the acclaimed Son of God, yet forsaken by God, does not find in this tradition of lament a soteriological or saving significance to that event. It is surprising that the vicariously redeeming suffering of the "servant of YHWH" in the *ebed* (servant) song of Isaiah 53 was not used, contrary to all expectation, as a frame for the passion narratives. "That there is almost no allusion to Isa. 53 in the earliest stage of the Passion narrative argues that this 'meditation on suffering' had not initially taken into account the salvific implication of Jesus' suffering and death."[6]

The liturgical and theological practice of the church has linked the text of Isaiah to the passion narrative as a "natural" fit, but it was *not* used in the Gospels as one would expect. The only explicit connection made between the vicarious motif of the song with Jesus' fate is found in 1 Peter 2:24-25, but not in the Gospels, which begs the question as to why this link was not made by the Gospel writers. There is little doubt

---

[3] Kathleen D. Billman and Daniel L. Migliore, *Rachel's Cry: Prayer of Lament and Rebirth of Hope* (Cleveland: United Church Press, 1999), 33.

[4] Ibid.

[5] Ibid., p. 31.

[6] Schillebeeckx, *Jesus*, 291

that they were familiar with the text. Did it simply not occur to them? This is implausible since so many, and more obscure, texts of the Hebrew Scriptures were claimed to have been fulfilled by Jesus. It is more likely that to interpret Jesus' death in the light of the servant's song of Isaiah 53 was considered preposterous specifically in its soteriological dimensions. Luke, the Gentile among the evangelists, comes closest and even quotes the song twice (Luke 22:37 and Acts 8:32-33), but avoids precisely that soteriological part of the song where the connection between suffering and vicarious redemption for our sake is asserted:

> But he was wounded for *our* transgressions, he was bruised for *our* inequities; upon him was the chastisement that made *us* whole, and with his stripes *we* are healed. All we like sheep have gone astray; we have turned everyone to his own way; and the LORD has laid on him the iniquity of *us* all. (Isa. 53:5-6)

Luke 22:37 quotes only verse 12 from Isaiah 53: "And he was counted among the lawless." In Acts 8:32-33, the quote from Isaiah 53:7-8 starts just *after* this conclusion from verse 6 ("...and the Lord has laid on him the iniquity of us all"), and Luke ends his quote just *before* the end of verse 8 ("stricken for the transgression of my people"), which implies redemptive surrogacy. Luke does not allow the song to cast Jesus' fate as a redemptive event; he quotes from the song but avoids with a surgeon's precision its soteriological lines.

Scholars[7] have detected in pre-Markan materials two conceptual streams or subtraditions of lament that only later merge, forming a basin within which a soteriological interpretation emerges, in a context already saturated by an apocalyptic ethos. But these streams themselves do not connect Jesus' passion and death to a salvific motif.

Traces of one stream can be found in a passage like Mark 8:31a and parallels: "The Son of [Humanity] must undergo great suffering, and be rejected...and be killed." The "must" (*dei*) in this passage is an inevitable imperative: *he has to!* What happened to Jesus is the fate of a true prophet

---

[7] See ibid., 282–94, for a detailed account of recent scholarship.

in a claim that goes back to Nehemiah 9:26: "they were disobedient and rebelled against you and cast your law behind their backs and killed your prophets." The motif identifies martyrdom as the mark of true prophecy. The apocalyptic overtones are defined by an imminent reversal of expectations due to the nearness of the parousia—the return of Jesus Christ.[8]

It was believed that the imminent advent of the Messiah would be marked by the simultaneous coming of the anti-Christ, with a bestiary of images inspired by Daniel 7 (and later taken up in Revelation 13).[9] In this context Jesus, who is persecuted and eventually killed, who is accused of apostasy, blasphemy, of being the anti-Messiah, the great Gainsayer (Matt. 12:24-32; 27:62-64; John 7:12), this Jesus is the one God truly vindicates and glorifies.

The world is out of joint; values are reversed. We find this well expressed in the rhetorical question of Stephen's speech before his own martyrdom: "Which of the prophets did your ancestors not persecute?" (Acts 7:52), and elsewhere (for example, in the Mark 12 parable of the wicked tenants). This would suggest that the death of a prophet, vindicated by God, would corroborate the truthfulness of the prophet's ministry.

So the death of Jesus would necessarily point back to his life. Martyrdom would vindicate the life and mission of the Righteous One, but such a death would not, could not, and should not be justified; it remains a tragic event, the outrageous price charged to the One who was righteous. The apocalyptic theme is well expressed in the reversal of Jesus' fate; what seems to be the case, a sinner condemned, reveals its opposite. The accused One is the true authority. The champion of the "true law" is the One with *exousia* (authority) who was killed by the false law, the false authority.

---

[8] I will later elaborate on what the term *apocalyptic* denotes and how we employ it. It suffices now to define it for our purpose not by a literary style (as in Daniel or Revelation) but by an ethos as denoting the expectation of the imminent coming of the Messiah in which a reversal of eons takes place under the sovereignty of God. See Richard E. Sturm, "Defining the Word 'Apocalyptic,'" in *Apocalyptic and the New Testament: Essays in Honor of J. L. Martyn*, ed. Joel Marcus and Marion Soards, (Sheffield: JSOT Press, 1989), 36; Ernst Käsemann, "Zur Thema der urchristlichen Apokalyptik," in *Exegetische Versuche und Besinnungen*, 2:105–06, n.1. For a summary of the recent debate, see Alexandra R. Brown, *The Cross and Human Transformation: Paul's Apocalyptic Word in 1 Corinthians* (Minneapolis: Fortress Press, 1995), 1–12.

[9] Schillebeeckx, *Jesus*, 278.

The second stream is still demarcated by the Jewish framework that characterized very early Christian theology. Traces of it can be found in Mark 9:31a and parallels: "The Son of [Humanity] is to be betrayed into human hands." The death of Jesus was interpreted as the fulfillment of prophecies: it had to happen. In the parallel passage of Luke 24:7, the "is to" (*dei*) is employed, suggesting a divine imperative. The words of Jesus himself according to Luke 24:25-26 attest: "Foolish people, and slow of heart to believe all that the prophets have spoken! Was it not necessary [*edei*, imperfect of *dei*] that the Christ should suffer these things and enter into his glory?"

This interpretation's authenticity can be traced to an ancient Aramaic play on words in the dictum: the Son of Humanity (*bene nasha*) must be (*dei*) delivered to the hands of humanity (*bar nasha*).[10] Paul's phrasing in 1 Corinthians 15:3-4 comes from a preexisting source with this subtradition of inevitability: "Christ died…in accordance with the scriptures." The tradition builds on the main source of lament prayers, the suffering of the righteous in wisdom literature.[11] Psalm 34:19a declares, "Many are the afflictions of the righteous."

What brings about the fate of the innocent victim? The difference between the two interpretations of Jesus' suffering and death—(*a*) the righteous one must be killed, and (*b*) the Son of Humanity must be handed over to the hands of humanity—is based on its cause. In the first it is the unfaithfulness of the people; the second suggests divine preordinance. In neither is a salvific or atoning content appended to the fate of the righteous. Why does the healer succumb to the most pernicious death? The scandal definitely remains and is aggravated by other evidence that cannot be easily explained away. For example, consider the fate of the one hanging on a tree as the accursed one of God (Deut. 21:23); Paul himself painfully recalls this text to his readers in Galatians 3:13. Further, Jesus' death took place in a space where God was thought to be absent. It was a space in which God's revelation would not occur, a place that could not witness to divine glory; it was an anti-epiphanic space, for it was the place of the skull.

[10] Joachim Jeremias, *Der Opfertod Jesu Christi* (Stuttgart: Calwer, 1963), 24; and Walter Zimmerli and Joachim Jeremias, *The Servant of God* (Naperville: A. R. Allenson, 1957), 102.
[11] Schillebeeckx, *Jesus*, 287.

These early attempts to frame the crucifixion as inevitability, brought about either by the unfaithfulness of the people or by a divine design, are both laden with Jewish prayer of lament and theological reflection on the suffering of the righteous that will come to fruition in an apocalyptic milieu. The religious underpinnings of these early traditions are probably why the Gospels assign more religious overtones to Jesus' trial than can be historically corroborated, leaving the impression that the Roman administration acted merely as an instrument in carrying out the execution. The Gospel writers emphasized the religious debasement of the Jewish leaders in order to vindicate their own religious experience and uprightness. While the Sanhedrin played a role in the process, historically Jesus' trial was primarily a political one as was the means of his execution. If the prevailing accusation against Jesus had been religious blasphemy, his fate would be that of Stephen: he would have been stoned, as stipulated in Numbers 15:32-36.

Soteriological Merger and the Apocalyptic

Before most of the Gospels were written, with the possible exception of Mark, salvation motifs were already finding their way into Christian circles. Ransom, sacrifice, punitive substitution, new covenant, and possibly also the *ebed* song of Isaiah 53 (certainly later in 1 Peter 2:24-25) are some with which we are familiar. Although sparse in its usage in pre-Synoptic and pre-Pauline material,[12] the origin of these soteriological motifs is found in the employment of the *hyper* formulae: he died for (*hyper*) us (*hemon*)/many (*pollon*).

The concept of a salvific interpretation came about when those two subtraditions merged. If in one of the subtraditions the unfaithfulness of the people is the source of the suffering of the Righteous One and in the other it is a divine disposition, once they are brought together the atoning motif is lost. If unfaithfulness *and* divine ordinance are merged as co-agents, then there are only two possibilities. In this co-agency either God works along with unfaithfulness (which would be malevolent), or

---

[12] See ibid., 291–94.

God's work is against the power of unfaithfulness. The first possibility would be apostasy. The second, leading to soteriological motifs, is the logical outcome. If God and the people are agents of the suffering of the Righteous One, then God's agency must be understood as an atoning act against treacherous people. God's act, although it seems to play into the hands of evil, is conceived as a way of subverting the actions of the evildoers.

Many early theologians used this motif ingeniously, even to suggest that Christ was the bait on the hook that caught the devil, a little sacrifice for a great reward. Later Latin theology in the West gave the atonement argument a juridical and more rational frame but kept the basic merger in place; the human sinful agency working with God's saving agency.[13] At this early stage of the merger of two subtraditions we see the apocalyptic framing the narrative.[14] Before we consider theological salvific motifs and atoning theories, however, we must focus on the context that prompted the emergence of these soteriological explanations. If this context is missing, as it often has been, the salvific meaning easily leads to domesticating the cross by removing it from historical actuality.

The apocalyptic context[15] allowed the marginal community of Christians within an already marginalized Palestinian environment (and across the Roman domain in scattered communities that were also socially, politically, and religiously marginalized) to understand themselves as the inheritors of a problematic divine election. To inhabit this margin, to be exiled from the center (religious, political, and economic), even to be accursed, is felt to be blessed to receive the sacred revelation. The places where the divine epiphany could not be imagined was reckoned as the really privileged place where apocalypse happens. The God that comes, the One who becomes present ("presence," from the Latin *prae-esse*, the precise meaning of the Greek *parousia*) is simultaneously manifested in God's most radical absence (from the Latin *ab-esse* and in Greek *apousia*). Such is then the advice of Jesus: if they tell you where or when he comes don't believe it, he comes in the uncanny image of a robber at night (Matt.

---

[13] See Gustaf Aulén, *Christus Victor* (New York: MacMillan, 1969).

[14] Brown, *The Cross and Human Transformation*, 59–64.

[15] See Käsemann, "Zur Thema der urchristlichen Apokalyptic."

24:43). Yes, even as a robber executed on the cross when midday turned into night (Mark 15:33)! This apocalyptic imagery and the frame that it provided allowed the Christian community to understand itself as the chosen of God in spite of and because of its unsightly appearance. It was into such a frame that the cross itself was drafted.

Bear in mind the location of the cross, the "place of the skull" (Golgotha in Hebrew, Calvary in Latin, *kranion* in Greek), outside the walls of the holy city. It is not even in *another* place, just outside Jerusalem. It is a place that is no place, which New Testament and other Greek authors refer to as *chora*, a place that is neither in nor out, yet simultaneously both. The time of day, noon, the hour of light, is turned into utter darkness. The curtain of the Temple, the demarcated space of the holy, is torn open from top to bottom. The Lord of Life is dead.

Only in the context of apocalyptic eschatology can we understand how the Christian faith could recognize the shame and the scandal of the cross at the same time it held the cross as the very center—more, as the *crux*—of Christian theology and piety. Without the apocalyptic frame, the scandal in which the cross is cast disappears. The message it entails, the *logos tou staurou*, can only be found where the world's *logos*—that is, the logic by which this world operates—breaks down. Here theology meets the end of its linguistic possibilities. It cannot reason itself out of the riddle. For our way of reasoning, this is an insurmountable paradox. Only grace through faith will join that which is out of joint and cannot be reasoned through. Nicolas of Cusa aptly called it *coincidentia oppositorum*, a coming upon of opposites.

The *logos tou staurou* is an incision through the assumed contiguity between rationality and divine wisdom. It defies any attempt to conclude meaning, for the boundary ground on which it stands is not fixed; it is semantically ambivalent and unsettled. At this unstable ground the apocalyptic ethos provides the frame for a new way of knowing. God's wisdom is to be received only *kata stauron*, according to the cross or from the perspective of the cross.[16] Read the Magnificat from this perspective, or the story of Jesus' birth in a manger, the King of Kings born in a barn in

---

[16] Brown, *The Cross and Human Transformation*, 8–9.

the midst of animals, flies, and manure. Look at Jesus' whole ministry with the marginalized, the destitute, the sick, possessed, and dispossessed (!), even the dead from this paradoxical viewpoint.

Humilitas and *Sublimitas*

The contrasts and movements of reversion are not only indicated by the biblical text; they reflect themselves in the texture of the biblical narrative creating a literary genre characterized by what Adolf von Harnack called a "pendulation" (*Pendelauschlag*) and Rudolf Bultmann described as a literature *sui generis*. This characterization is not exclusive to theologians and biblical scholars. In his monumental commentary on the development of Western literature, *Mimesis,* Erich Auerbach (an exiled German Jew writing in Istanbul during World War II), presents the distinctiveness of biblical literature, written in Hebrew or Greek. According to Auerbach, biblical literature, particularly in the Gospels, manifests this combination of opposites. The result is a mingling of two literary styles never before mixed. He argues:

> In antique theory, the sublime and elevated style was called *sermo gravis* or *sublimis*; the low style was *sermo remissus* or *humilis*; the two had to be kept strictly separated. In the world of Christianity, on the other hand, the two are merged, especially in Christ's Incarnation and Passion, which realize and combine *sublimitas* and *humilitas* in overwhelming measure.[17]

Auerbach continues, showing that "this mingling of styles [is] inconceivable [in classic Greek literature],…it was rooted from the beginning in the character of Jewish-Christian literature."[18] Uniquely in biblical literature, the "sublime influence of God reaches so deeply into the everyday that the two realms of the sublime and everyday are not actually unseparated but basically inseparable."[19]

---

[17] Erich Auerbach, *Mimesis: The Representation of Reality in Western Literature* (Princeton: Princeton University Press, 1953), 151.

[18] Ibid., 41.

[19] Ibid., 22–23.

Auerbach's research reveals the milieu from which biblical literature emerges and how particularly the account of Christ's passion reflects itself in the hybrid style of the biblical text with its conflation of opposites:

> [T]he principle of mixed styles makes its way into the writings of the Fathers from the Judaeo-Christian tradition....the King of Kings was treated as a low criminal,...he was mocked, spat upon, whipped and nailed to the cross—a new *sermo humilis* is born, a low style, such as would properly only be applicable to comedy, but which now encroaches upon the deepest and the highest, the sublime and the eternal.[20]

The early twentieth-century scholar Martin Dibelius described this conflation of *humilitas* and *sublimitas* that first distinguished biblical literature, in particular the Gospels, as little or low literature (*Klein-Literatur*).[21] Christians claim it conveys nothing less than divine revelation. To say that the lowest can be the vessel of the highest is not a strong enough statement. It would be more correct to say that only the lowest can encompass the highest; only the last can be the first; only the lost can be found.

This statement has definite consequences for the whole of theology and finds expression in the two most elaborated early Christians doctrines: the two natures of Christ and the Trinity. Both doctrines should be framed and receive their meaning in the context of the experience of Jesus' followers as they came to terms with his crucifixion. The implications of the incarnation culminating in the cross provided the main problem in the dispute that brought four centuries of debate over the person Christ, synthesized in the Formula of Chalcedon in 451.

It was the unabashed affirmation of God's embodiment, summarized in the formula *vere Deus et vere homo* (truly God and truly human), that would finally etch into theology the paradox revealed by the cross: God

---

[20] Ibid., 72.

[21] Martin Dibelius, *Die Formgeschichte des Evangeliums*, 3rd ed. (J.C.B. Mohr, 1959), 1–2. Although Dibelius uses *Klein-Literatur* consistently as a *terminus technicus* the English renders it in several ways: ("unpretentious literature," "lowly form of literature") or omits the notion altogether. See Dibelius, *From Tradition to Gospel* (Cambridge: James Clark, 1971), 1–2.

dies. Let us summarize the argument the incarnation entails, because it is the necessary background for the understanding of the emergence of trinitarian language, which in turn is an attempt to give a narrative form to the paradoxical utterances and fragmented language that describe the cross.

Incarnation

The doctrine of the incarnation is a distinctively Christian feature. Other religions have notions of incarnation, like the Hindu avatars, but uniquely Christian is the understanding that God's incarnation or embodiment is not a lofty display of God's majesty but a descent into the most deprived level of the human condition, down to abject death itself. God's solidarity reaches the depth of creation and is subjected to the humility of its most depraved condition.

Early in the history of Christian theology it was emphatically established that God became fully and truly human. Today this might sound like a truism, something learned by heart; we don't realize that there was something appalling about it. In the early church a dispute emerged and the alternative options of Docetism and Ebionism were offered. In a more nuanced manner, the same options were continuously discussed. For example, some theologians (Apollinarius is the classical example) would admit that God's embodiment was real, but Christ could not really have had a human mind, for a human mind changes and has needs and wills, and this could not have been possible since Christ is divine. Gregory of Nazianzen in the fourth century gave the classical response that remains until today one of the treasures of Christian theology: "If anyone has put their trust in Him [Christ] as a human being without a human mind, they are bereft of mind, and quite unworthy of salvation. For that which He has not assumed He has not healed; but that which is united to His Godhead is also saved."[22] Salvation and liberation is only possible, said Gregory, if God is united and identified with that which needs salvation

---

[22] Gregory Nazianzen, Ep. CI in *Nicene and Post-Nicene Fathers* (Peabody, Mass.: Hendrickson, 1995) 7:440.

and liberation. And if nothing is outside of the reach of God, then God has been there and is there where salvation is needed.

Yet even more important is the dimension this embodiment encompasses. Early Christian theology emerged within a worldview in which nature was not exploited and abused as it is today.[23] Contrary to the common modern assumption that the Christian incarnation reached only the top of the chain of being, humanity, and was not radical enough to include the whole of nature, Christian theology then understood most decisively the human nature not to be at the top but rather at the bottom of the scale of corruption and abuse. So the incarnation affirms that God reached out not to the top of what has been called the "chain of being," but the very bottom, the most distressed level of all of God's creation, implying that all the rest is encompassed as well. This is what the fourth-century Saint Athanasius attests to:

> Now, if they ask, Why then did [God] not appear by means of other and nobler parts of creation, and use some nobler instrument, as the sun, or moon, or stars, or fire, or air, instead of a human merely? let them know that the Lord came not to make a display, but to heal and teach those who were suffering... nothing in creation had gone astray with regards to their notions of God, save humans only.[24]

In the fifth century Bishop Cajus Caelius Sedulius of Achaia wrote in a strophe of a hymn:

> Blessed creator of all there is
> In the body of a servant fit
> So that flesh the flesh liberates
> And loses nothing that he makes.[25]

---

[23] The word *ecology* used in the sense of studying the human impact on the environment was used for the first time only in the 1950s.

[24] Athanasius, *De Incarnatione Verbi* (§ 43), in *Nicene and Post-Nicene Fathers*, 4:59.

[25] See Hermann Brandt, *Gottes Gegenwart in Lateinamerika: Inkarnation als Leitmotiv der Befreiungstheologie* (Hamburg: Steinmann & Steinmann, 1992), V–VI. Luther in *WA* 35, 150 quotes the original (which he later translates): "Beatus auctor saeculi / servile corpus induit, / Ut carne carnem liberans / ne perderet quos condidit."

A similar argument is made in the Lutheran tradition with the notion that the finite is capable of the infinite (*finitum capax infiniti*). This continues the thinking of Gregory and Athanasius. It became a distinctive Lutheran position due to disputes with the Reformed wing of the Reformation. Luther and the Lutheran reformers rejected the interpretation of the creedal formulation that "seated at the right hand of the Father" meant a particular location. Yet apart from this confessional dispute more was at stake.

The expression that indicates that Christ is at the right hand of the Triune God means that Christ as God's "right hand" is everywhere.[26] How can that be and what does it imply? Luther and the authors of the Confessions distinguished three modes of Christ's presence. The first was called the *corporeal* mode, referring to Jesus of Nazareth in his historical existence. The second is called the *spiritual* mode, as when Christ can enter any reality without vacating space, as when he came out of the tomb or walked through close doors. This is also his mode of presence in the sacramental bread and wine by which real presence "in, with, and under" the elements can be affirmed without appealing to a transformation of the substance of the elements, that is, without transubstantiation. The third mode of presence, which is called the *heavenly* mode, is the one in which Christ by sharing God's infinity and omnipresence is "far, far beyond things created, as far as God transcends them."[27] By virtue of the incarnational unity between the infinite and the finite, however, Christ must be at the same time as deep in and as near to all created things as God is in them so that Christ's body can be anywhere because "he is and can be wherever God is and that everything is full of Christ through and through, even according to his humanity."[28]

---

[26] *Formula of Concord, Solid Declaration*, art. VII in *The Book of Concord*, ed. Robert Kolb and Timothy Wengert (Minneapolis: Fortress Press, 2000), 609.

[27] Ibid., 610.

[28] Ibid., art. VIII, 631. All the above references in the *Book of Concord* are citations of Luther's "Confession on the Supper" (1528). Cf. Martin Luther, "Confession Concerning Christ's Supper (1528)," *Luther's Works* vol. 37 *Word and Sacrament III*, ed. and trans. Robert H. Fischer (Philadelphia: Fortress Press, 1961), 151–372.

"Even according to his humanity" is the definite strike against any kind of "spiritualizing" God's presence. The consequence is that although the corporeal mode of Christ's presence is limited in time and space, Christ's *embodiment* ("even according to his humanity") is not limited to that corporeal mode of presence in Jesus of Nazareth. Christ is everywhere, closer to everything created than these things are to themselves. God's embodiment through Christ encompasses the world. That is true even in the midst of God's radical identification with the most deprived of the human condition. In the words of literary critic Michael Hardt:

> The plenitude of materiality, the fullness of existence is divine. But why should we speak about divinity here, when the form of God has been completely emptied out, abandoned? Because divinity marks the essential vitality of existence. The surfaces of the world are charged with a powerful intensity. Divinity resides precisely in the margins or thresholds of things, at their limits, passionate and exposed, as if surrounding them with a halo.[29]

Such a radical emphasis on the incarnation implies, as Luther acknowledges, that the incarnation of Christ must always be spoken of in the past tense, and in the present as well as in the future: "from eternity [Christ] is born, he is always [being] born."[30] If this holds promise for understanding the connection between the passion of Christ and the passion of the world, it sharpens the paradox of the theology of the cross, because it follows that God's death (in the cross of Jesus) was a death then, is now, and will be in the future. How can we address such implications for theological language? This is where trinitarian discourse comes into play.

---

[29] Michael Hardt, "Exposure: Pasolini in the Flesh," in *A Shock to Thought: Expresson after Deleuze and Guattari*, ed. Brian Massumi (London: Routledge, 2002), 79.

[30] "*Quicquid ab aeterno nascitur, semper nascitur.*" *WA* 39/II, 293.

Trinity

The formulation of the doctrine of the Trinity, though awkward and extremely cumbersome when subjected to logical[31] or analogical[32] arguments, was the most accomplished effort to provide an answer to this question within the limits of human language. This doctrine is not the logical result of a systematization of the scant and inconclusive inferences to the Trinity or the few trinitarian formulae in the New Testament. It also does not ensue from the inventive early christological and trinitarian debates and speculations. Rather, it is a direct result of the apocalyptic reading of the crucifixion of Jesus, which the Lutheran tradition has so well and so scandalously expressed in the notion (now jargon) of the death of God, or in the classic saying: *Nemo contra deum nisi deus ipse* (nothing against God but God's own self).[33]

The problem the early Christians were dealing with is similar to the legendary riddle posed by the pre-Socratic Eleatic philosophers five centuries before Christ: If God is almighty, is God powerful enough to create a rock so big that God cannot move it? Either answer, yes or no, contradicts the assumed attribute of the all-powerfulness of God. The early Christians had a comparable riddle; they inverted it with an astonishing "logical" result: Can God be so powerful as to surrender all power? And the answer was yes! They truly shifted the riddle from the question to the answer! All attempts at coming to terms with the humiliating experience of the cross find their basis in this affirmative answer to the riddle. We find that answer for the first time, formulated with astonishing sharpness, in 1 Corinthians 1:18: "For the message of the cross [*logos tou staurou*] is foolishness to those who are perishing, but to us who are being saved it is the power of God."

[31] The most celebrated logical rendition of the Trinity is Hegel's, which can be summarized in his formula: the identity of identity and nonidentity. G. W. F. Hegel, *Werke* (Frankfurt a/M: Suhrkamp, 1970), 2:96.

[32] Analogical arguments sustain that we find in human experience traces of "triunity" (*vestigia trinitatis*), as in Augustine's analogy of memory, intelligence, and will.

[33] The expression is of unknown origin, but was popularized by Wolfgang von Goethe, who used it as the epigraph for the fourth part of his *Dichtung und Wahrheit* (Leipzig: Hermann Seemann Nachfolger, 1903), 459.

That God has within Godself the compassionate capability of being the denial of God lies at the core of trinitarian formulations. The doctrine of the Trinity often went out of control in fanciful speculations, which led Melanchthon to his famous admonition: "The mystery of the Godhead we should rather worship, than investigate."[34] There is something unstable and counterintuitive at the core of the Trinity as we try to conceive it. Gregory Nazianzen even uses the Greek word *stasis*, in the sense of "insurrection" (as in Mark 15:7), "riot" (Acts 19:40), "rebellion," "being at variance with," to describe what defies neat conceptualization. God, he writes, "is not limited to one Person, for it is possible for Unity if at variance (*stasis*) with itself come into a condition of plurality....Therefore Unity having from all eternity arrived by motion at Duality, found its rest in Trinity."[35] We have found a way to express what seems to be a logical quagmire. But how are we to make sense of this relationship between the divine and its own negation?

Communication

All the different and elaborate trinitarian discussions should be seen as a corollary to the attempt to provide some intelligibility, though unstable, to this apocalyptic subtext in which God encompasses God's own negation; God embraces all, even death and hell, as the Creed would finally radicalize it. Gregory of Nazianzen, as we have seen, formulated this conviction by saying that "that which is not assumed is not redeemed." Even hell is not beyond God's encompassing and gracious embrace.

From this perspective, the cross of God's forsakenness (in both senses: the cross that God forsakes and the cross in which God is forsaken) represents that which cannot be regulated, except by a third that is not spoken but which makes the confession of this implausible deity, the one who entails its own denial and forsakenness, possible: the Holy Spirit. This third allows the opposites to remain in tension. The radical differences between life and death, infinity and finitude, are reconciled by a radical

---

[34] Philip Melanchthon, *Loci Communes 1521* (Gütersloh: Gerd Mohn, 1993), 18.

[35] Gregory Nazianzen, Third Theological Oration: "On the Son" II, in *Nicene and Post-Nicene Fathers*, 7:301.

affirmation that in the passion of Jesus' own forsakenness there is God's compassion. In the post-Reformation interpretation of the Chalcedonian *communicatio idiomatum* (the communication of the attributes or linguistic expressions of the two natures of Christ) one of the ways it happens is called *genus tapeinoticum* (the genre of humbleness), by which the attributes of Jesus' human nature (including his suffering and death) can be divine attributes.[36] This is the work of the Spirit, which we could cautiously say implicates God in and with the fate of the world.

The Spirit, which etymologically means "breath" or "wind" (*ruah* in Hebrew or *pneuma* in Greek) is that which speaks, for if it is the subject of the act of speech itself it cannot be objectified by our own language. It is the breath that we exhale which allows us to utter words, even and above all those words that defy our comprehension. That which makes speech possible cannot be spoken about; it is what makes it possible for us to speak and confess even the implausible. Paul expressed this well when he distinguished idolatry from the gift of the Spirit. Idols, Paul explains in 1 Corinthians 12, do not speak, through them the Spirit does not breathe. The idol is a fixation of the sight that blinds us to everything else; its arrests the gaze. The idol, even if it were a crucifix, is the stable image of an unstable reality. It soothes and mesmerizes, but does not move us. The Spirit is that which makes it possible for us to utter what we know is foolish. This is why Paul, who said the *logos tou staurou* is foolishness, can also say: "no one can say 'Jesus is Lord' except by the Holy Spirit" (1 Cor. 12:3). Centuries of Christian confession of this formula have obscured and domesticated the original astounding effect of its meaning. For Paul and his contemporaries, to say that a marginal man condemned to disgraceful death on a cross is Lord (*kurios*, the title of gods and emperors) demanded a language that defied anything then regarded plausible. This is the work of the Holy Spirit, which "bear[s] witness with [*summarturein*—"conspires" is a plausible translation] our spirit" (Rom. 8:16).

---

[36] Luther had already said it in less technical language: "Thus it is rightly and truly said: God is born, was nursed or suckled, lay in the crib, felt cold, walked, stood, fell, wandered, ate, drank, suffered, died, etc." *Tischreden*, VI:68, 18–40.

The Innocence of the Flesh

In the attempt to find a language fitting to describe the cross event in the life of God, the scandal of foolishness still remains. It remains thus to this day. Consider these lines from contemporary Brazilian poet Adélia Prado. In a disconcerting manner she renews the scandal, conflating love sublime with profane and coarse language. Prado takes the reader away from a slumbering sublimation and enchantment that so often mists over the passion narrative. The poem is entitled "The Feast of the Body of God."

Like a ripe tumor
poetry beats painfully,
announcing the passion:
Oh crux ave, spes unica
Oh passiones tempore.
Jesus has a pair of buttocks!
More than Yahweh in the mountain
this revelation prostrates me.
Oh mystery, mystery,
hanging in a tree
the human body of God.
It is proper of sex the air
that in the old deities I undrape,
as in children supposedly
perverted and debauched.
In this consists the crime,
to picture a woman in orgasm
and say: behold the face of sin.
For centuries and centuries

demons squabbled
in blinding us with this.
And your body in the cross suspended.
And your body in the cross stripped:
>look at me.
I adore you, oh my savior
who passionately reveals me
the innocence of the flesh.
Exposing yourself like a fruit
in this tree of execration
what you say is love,
love of the body, love.[37]

Much more can be said about the doctrines of the two natures and the Trinity, but this is a necessary beginning for understanding an often obtuse language; it is an attempt to say what language cannot convey and reason fails to muster. It has been said that the doctrine of the Trinity, more than *having* a point, *is* the point.[38] This misses the crux of the matter, that indeed it has, above all, *a point*: the cross of Jesus Christ.

[37] Adélia Prado, *Poesia Reunida* (São Paulo: Siciliano, 1991), 279.

[38] Robert Jenson, "The Point of Trinitarian Theology," in Christoph Schwöbel, ed., *Trinitarian Theology Today: Essays on Divine Being and Act* (Edinburgh: T & T Clark, 1995), 43.

God against God
Reformation, Then and Now

Crux sola est nostra theologia.
Martin Luther

Cross as Tribulation

Martin Luther describes what makes a preacher and a theologian in the preface to the publication of his German texts in 1539.[1] Luther here breaks from the popular threefold medieval rules for theologizing—*lectio*, *oratio*, *contemplatio*—and introduces one of his own: *oratio*, *meditatio*, *tentatio*. Luther's schema begins with *oratio*, which is more than prayer; it is all God-talk, talk of and to God when one knows that reason will not suffice. Second is *meditatio*—in which he includes *lectio*—which is not limited to meditation in the internal sense but is also "external," hence engaging others in reflection.

Luther does not follow the third medieval rule, *contemplatio*, but instead he brings up a very different and original concept, *tentatio*, which becomes the foremost—the "touchstone" he calls it—and the

[1] Martin Luther, "Preface to the Wittenberg Edition of Luther's German Writings (1539)," *Luther's Works* vol. 34, *Career of the Reformer IV*, ed. Lewis W. Spitz, trans. Robert H. Heitner (Philadelphia: Fortress Press, 1960), 285–88.

last characteristic of theological reflection. *Tentatio* is the testing and tribulation one undergoes when doing what a theologian of the cross is supposed to do, that is, say the thing for what it is.[2] In his divergence from the medieval scheme and use of the Latin word *tentatio*, Luther clearly intends to call the reader's attention, familiar with the traditional formula, to the change. The word *tentatio* means "trial," "test," "being under attack." It is frequently used to describe the effects of an illness. The English word *temptation*, its primary meaning "enticement," just does not convey *tentatio* accurately.[3] Luther translates it to German as *Anfechtung*, which conveys "tribulation," "being upon a fight," "on trial," "caught in the ordeal of being tested." *Anfechtung* describes the pain and despair one feels with the fear and *Angst* of approaching a terrible error, of being driven to the edge. In *Anfechtung* one is not assisted by the approval of others but despised and criticized. Luther claimed that this is the only way to get to the theological truth; he concluded with irony: "I myself (if you permit me, mere mouse-dirt, to be mingled with pepper) am deeply indebted to my papists that through the devil's raging they have beaten, oppressed, and distressed me so much. That is to say, they have made a fairly good theologian of me, which I would not have become otherwise."[4] Luther's third precept grows out of his understanding of the theology of the cross: a theology being done by those afflicted, assailed, oppressed, and on trial. It is a certain practice (*usus*); a way of doing theology, a disposition that grows out of that very experience of *tentatio*. Theology of the cross as *Anfechtung* is by definition the opposite of fatalism or triumphalism; instead it is the practice of stepping into the middle of a battle against suffering.

---

[2] Joachim Tack, "Living and Structured Spirituality," in *Between Vision and Reality: Lutheran Churches in Transition*, ed. Wolfgang Greive (Geneva: Lutheran World Federation, 2001), 430.

[3] In Greek, *peirasmos* can have both the sense of trial (e.g., Gal. 4:14) but also of enticement (e.g., 1 Tim. 6:9).

[4] Martin Luther, "Preface to the Wittenberg Edition of Luther's German Writings (1539)," *Luther's Works* vol. 34, *Career of the Reformer IV*, ed. Lewis W. Spitz, trans. Robert H. Heitner (Philadelphia: Fortress Press, 1960), 287–88.

The Justice of God

Luther's well-known quest was to find a merciful God. Behind that quest is a problem that is no longer self-evident. Why was it not taken for granted that God is merciful? Is this a question of Luther's age and not ours? Are we not much more concerned today with lack of faith than with a faith afflicted by a terrifying God? Modern piety, with its benevolent God and "sweet Jesus," has made Luther's dilemma itself seem senseless or at least anachronistic. Reflecting on modern sensibilities, German theologian Heinz Eduard Tödt told the 1970 Evian assembly of the Lutheran World Federation that Luther's concern was the quest of a medieval monk overburdened by a sense of guilt that the modern mind can no longer understand.[5]

Then again, we no longer live in the optimistic 1960s or 1970s. The recent reissuing of indulgences by the Vatican (shortly after the "Joint Declaration on the Doctrine of Justifications" was signed in 1999 by the Vatican and the Lutheran World Federation); the number of U.S. Roman Catholic bishops rallying against a presidential candidate who was one of their own flock in favor of a born-again Methodist; evangelical Christians by the millions convinced that the rapture is about to leave the majority of us behind—all of these indicate a broader cultural trend. These are signals of a new sense of condemnation and affliction. On the other end of the present cultural spectrum, such a sense of condemnation might be illustrated by references to God as the "cosmic child abuser,"[6] the one who requires the sacrifice of the divine child, bringing back something similar to Luther's own quest for a merciful God, a context that produced these lines by Catherine of Siena a century and a half earlier:

Like a loving, injured God
My father looked threatening at me.

---

[5] *Sent into the World: The Proceedings of the Fifth Assembly of the Lutheran World Federation, Evian, France, July 14–24, 1970*, ed. LaVern K. Grosc (Minneapolis: Augsburg, 1971), 32.

[6] The expression was coined by Rita Nakashima Brock; see her essay "And a Little Child Will Lead Us," in Joanne Carlson Brown and Carole R. Bohn, eds., *Christianity, Patriarchy, and Abuse: A Feminist Critique* (Cleveland: Pilgrim Press, 1989), 53, 61 n. 13.

Yet had he stretched out both hands—
God against God
    (she takes a small crucifix from her breast and kisses it).
Rescue me, save me,
My Jesus, whom I follow, from his arm…
Rescue me, save me from my father,
and his love, his tyranny.[7]

Luther's struggle was unlike Catherine's in that it was not to evade the God of wrath by appealing to the image of Jesus, the eternal divine child. The Reformer's quest led to what he regarded as the central point of his anguish: What is the justice of God—*iustitia dei*? Luther's question is not the traditional question of theodicy: How can *we* justify evil in the world God created? His question is not anthropocentric, but theocentric: What does God regard as justice? Luther's torments, he finally realized, had been the product of a question that had gone unexamined for centuries: How can God be just and still be a loving God?

The most famous response to the question of divine justice was offered in Anselm's eleventh-century book entitled *Cur Deus Homo* ("Wherefore God Became Human"). Anselm's answer was one of the most ingenious, elegant, and logical arguments ever produced in theology. A brief summary is necessary to understand the source of Luther's tribulations.

For Anselm humans are sinful, so much so that they do not even realize the gravity of their condition. Sin is failure to give God the honor that is due to God. The result is condemnation. The divine loving will is to save, but how is a just God to save and show God's love without infringing upon the principle of justice? Since only God is capable of giving God the honor due and humans alone must make the payment, God sends the co-eternal Son as a human being, but one without sin. Being God, Christ is able to give God due honor, and being a human make the proper payment, suffering the condemnation we deserve. Anselm's argument relies on a fundamental juridical principle of old: the *suum cuique* (to each what to each is due), which means that if we have a debt, we either have

---

[7] Cited by Jürgen Moltmann, *The Crucified God* (Minneapolis: Fortress Press, 1993), 159.

to be punished or we need to satisfy the debt by paying it (*aut poena aut satisfactio*). Given this presupposition to the question, Anselm's was indeed a convincing response.

Just a generation later, Peter Abelard, spelled out a fatal problem in Anselm's argument by carrying the *suum cuique* to its logical conclusions. If for a relatively minor sin of failing to give due honor to God such sacrifice and punishment was required, who will now make the payment for humanity's having killed the very Son of God? Luther kept questions like these burning inside of him. Anselm offered one answer, but neither Abelard nor Luther followed suit. Abelard resolved the problem by evading the question of justice and affirming God's love as so deep that it is with us up to the point of our death; and by Christ's example love is awakened in us, freeing us from sin.

But for Luther the question of justice could not be evaded and the passion and crucifixion of Jesus further compounded the problem of our guilt. Abelard's criticism could only have deepened the anxiety of the young monk: we have done it, are we not to pay for it accordingly? Luther was tormented as long as he sought an answer to this problem. Meanwhile he raised a new set of questions that eventually led him to an answer: Should the unquestioned juridical presupposition of Anselm be more closely examined? Is God's justice ruled by the *suum cuique* principle?

More than a decade after Luther found the answer that gave him peace,[8] we have his mature exposition of his discovery. In his 1528 lectures on Isaiah 53 (which curiously contains the song of the vicarious servant of YHWH that the Gospels refrained from using as a frame for the passion narrative), Luther provides this intriguing definition of justice: "Behold the new definition of justice [*definitionem novam iusticiae*]: justice is the knowledge of Christ [*iusticia est cognicio Christi*]."[9] Some observations are here required.

---

[8] For a summary account of the convoluted debate about the breakthrough in the discovery of what God's justice means, see Alistair McGrath, *Luther's Theology of the Cross* (Oxford: Basil Blackwell, 1985), 95–147.

[9] *WA* 31/II, 439, 19f.; Martin Luther, "Isaiah 53:11," *Luther's Works* vol. 17 *Lectures on Isaiah 40–66*, ed. Hilton C. Oswald, trans. Herbert J. Bouman (St. Louis: Concordia, 1972), 230.

A first decisive element here is that the genitive in *cognicio Christi* is double: it is to know about Christ (objective genitive) and also to have the knowledge Christ had (subjective genitive). In this sense, it means to have the relationship to and intimacy with the One in heaven that Christ had, the One he called *Abba*, Father. To know that Christ came to be in our stead in relation to God also means that we are allowed to be in Christ's own stead. This is what Luther meant in his often-quoted reference to believers being "Christs."[10]

It is in the same context of the commentary on Isaiah 53 that Luther talks about how this is accomplished: it is a "wonderful exchange" (*mirabilem mutacionem*). And the exchange goes both ways, Christ in our stead and we in his! For the Reformer the flaw in the old question was that in it Christ took our place, yet we did not take his. This means that justice might be done *for* us but not *in* us. For Luther this is sophistry, which he detects in the implicit use of the *suum cuique* it presupposes: "The sophists say that righteousness is the fixed will to render to each his own."[11]

What Luther points to as a "new definition" (*definitionem novam*) is the second decisive element here. In relationship to what is this "new" defined? The Reformer knew—as anyone of his time with a standard higher education knew—that the *old* and classic definition of justice (as rendered by Cicero, Pliny the Elder, and others, yet probably older) was the proverbial *suum cuique* ("to each what to each is due") to which he refers in the same text.[12] This was the prevailing, broadly accepted, and unquestioned concept of justice. For Luther to suggest a "new" concept of justice was a scandalous subversion of the venerable maxim. His radical rephrasing says, "to us what is not due to us [but comes as a gift]," as well as "to others what is not due to them [but is freely given]." Such is the new concept of justice, the free gift of God surrendering Godself to us. Such is the meaning of Christ revealed ironically in his cross, the ultimate self-giving of God.

[10] *WA* 45, 532, 5–9; Martin Luther, "Chapter 14," *Luther's Works* vol. 24, *Sermons on the Gospel of St. John, Chapters 14–16*, ed. Jaroslav Pelikan, trans. Martin H. Bertram (St. Louis: Concordia, 1961), 78.

[11] *LW* 17:229; *WA* 31/II, 439, 5–6: *Iusticia est constans voluntas reddenti cuique, quod suum est.*

[12] *WA* 31/II, 439, 5f.; *LW* 17:229.

The justice of God that is Christ has two interrelated aspects. First, it entails the grace of God toward us in the midst of our condition, declaring us righteous and not simply supplementing or mending the shortcomings we have. We are made whole in the midst of our brokenness. Nothing else is meant by the formula *simul iustus et peccator*. Second, this justice is also done by disclosing wickedness in the systems of knowledge and power that rule this fallen world, making us aware of evil to which we are otherwise blind. The new justice, the knowledge of Christ in this second aspect, can only be seen as foolishness because it reveals the "wisdom" that rules a fallen world. The power of Christ is indeed weakness. Jesus himself was trapped in the rule of the fallen world and so this understanding concedes that we are unable to fight these powers—or so it seems. It seems so because this power and wisdom is still hidden under its opposite and "no eye has seen, nor ear heard, nor the human heart conceived." (1 Cor. 2:9).

Such a reading of Luther's text allows us to realize what Gustaf Aulén and others already have noticed:[13] Luther is struggling with language in order to bring to light something new, some good news, while remaining a child of his old world with its "reasons" in all the commonly recognized institutional realms. His attack on philosophy (with its "reason"), the economic system (with its "markets"), jurisprudence (with its "justice"), the territorial states (with their "politics"), and the church (with its "hierarchies") was not intended to remodel them. The Reformation was not about "reforming," as when one restores a building or remodels a house. It is about a *new* formation. But how can we understand this?

The Reformer was well aware of the inefficacy of interweaving the new with the old (Luke 5:36). He wanted to find or even provoke a crack, a crisis, in the systems that controlled and organized the institutions basic to a general medieval consensus: *ecclesia, oeconomia,* and *politia*. The "new" definition not only redresses the old, mending the fractures; it is something new, a new that is good (*euangelion*), a gift that keeps on giving;

---

[13] Anders Nygren, *Meaning and Method* (Philadelphia: Fortress Press, 1972), 243–64; Dennis Bielfeldt, "Luther on Language," *Lutheran Quarterly* XVI, no. 2 (Summer 2000): 195–220; Vítor Westhelle, "Communication and the Transgression of Language in Martin Luther," *Lutheran Quarterly* XVI, no. 1 (Spring 2003): 1–27.

it cracks the surfaces, opens up the wounds behind the mask of normality, and reveals the crisis. For those of no faith this is the concession of a defeat, the foolishness of admitting the power of the enemy. That is the message of the cross: the admission of a defeat which is the very gate that leads to victory.

In our pursuit to be righteous—to have our due share and pay our dues, which does not succeed—the justice of Christ breaks in and fragments the systems of the world, its philosophy, ecclesial structures, legal rules— in short, the earthly economies and régimes. Instead of fighting them with their own rules and weapons, the justice of Christ transgresses their wisdom and legislations. The possibilities of divine justice in the midst of this world manifest themselves precisely where these economies and régimes break down or are transgressed. How is that done? By showing that behind every one of the ruling systems or the earthly régimes there is an implicit promise that they will deliver salvation, safety, property, freedom and emancipation, and thus a disguised failure. They hide their failures by demanding more compliance. And we comply in the belief of the reasonableness of their request.

Finite Justice

This is still a negative if not apocalyptic definition of justice, however. It is not enough to know about the power of fragmentation. We must also ask what brings about justice, finite justice, in the midst of everyday life and in spite of the powers and the knowledges (*epistemes*) that rule the world with their empty promises. It is not difficult to find the fragmenting and apocalyptic force of irony in Luther. But is there also an analogical move whose continuities counterbalance the fragmenting force of irony? Is there a compromise through which we can live in this interim before the apocalypse, or in the midst of it? There must be something that made Luther say that even if he knew the world would end tomorrow, he would plant a tree.

Luther scholarship has answered this question with the so-called two-kingdoms doctrine. Most of the discussion that dominated Luther scholarship from the 1930s through the 1970s was plagued by a Platonic dualism between a spiritual sphere and an earthly one. One commentator declared the discussion so confusing that it looked like a labyrinth whose architect had lost the blueprint in the midst of construction.[14] A careful examination of this question and an insightful Ariadne's thread out of the labyrinth is offered by a little-known but important work by Swedish theologian Gustav Törnvall.[15] Breaking with the approach to the two-kingdoms doctrine that aligned the kingdoms to spiritual and secular institutions—an approach that has dominated discussion about justification and justice in Lutheran scholarship—Törnvall appeals to a functional interpretation of Luther's categories that refer to what is being discussed under "two kingdoms."

Pointing to Luther's inconsistent use of terms to refer to these realities,[16] Törnvall argues that the frequently institutional and essentialist language only reveals Luther's celebrated concern with being concrete in his imagery.[17] The two governances or régimes are fundamentally expressions of the Creator/creature theme in God's self-revelation, through the masks of God (*larvae dei*), the invisible Word of God (*verbum dei*), and the visible world. The result, for Törnvall, is that the two kingdoms are both functional aspects of God's revelation: a kingdom of listening (*Hörreich*) and a kingdom of seeing (*Sehereich*).[18] They are perspectives or dimensions of the single act of God's creation and revelation, and only derivatively institutional realities.[19] Hence, the basic distinction operative in Luther's

---

[14] For a brief summary of this debate, see Vítor Westhelle, "The Word and the Mask: Revisiting the Two-Kingdoms Doctrine," in *The Gift of Grace: The Future of Lutheran Theology*, ed. Niels Henrik Gregersen, Bo Holm, Ted Peters, and Peter Widman (Minneapolis: Fortress Press, 2005), 167–78.

[15] Gustaf Törnvall, *Geistliches und weltliches Regiment bei Luther* (München: Kaiser, 1947).

[16] Ibid., 94–95. He quotes thirty-eight different couples of terms Luther used to frame the distinction.

[17] Ibid., 38.

[18] Although there are similarities with the Platonic distinction between *to araton* (the visible) and *to noeton* (the intelligible), in Plato the distinction is about perception of the real and intellection of the essence, the former being a shadow image of the latter, while for Luther the distinction is about two ways of perceiving while rejecting the speculative pursuance of the essential. In other words, the Platonic distinction is ontological, Luther's is epistemological.

[19] Cf. ibid., 17. In his interpretation of the law in Luther, Gerhard Forde follows a similar insight: "'law' is to be taken in a functional rather than a material sense." See his locus on "Christian Life" in Carl Braaten and Robert Jenson, eds., *Christian Dogmatics*, 2 vols. (Philadelphia: Fortress Press, 1984), 2:400.

thinking, at least since the Heidelberg Disputation of 1518,[20] is the one between the visible and the Word, between creature and Creator, the outer and the inner, between what the senses register and reason draws together and what grace reveals to the spirit. How can the visible and the audible be related in the midst of existence, and how do we recognize them in their relationship?

Irony

Between these sets of categories there is a paradoxical and asymmetric relationship that Luther uses to formulate his understanding of God's revelation. It is "paradoxical" in that one (the visible) points to the other (the Word) but is thereby simultaneously negated or dissimulated. He rejects exclusively analogical reasoning while keeping open some room for analogical correspondence. Luther's mode of argument never does away with analogy; at the same time he constantly inserts elements of irony to disturb the tranquil realm of analogical correspondence. It is impossible to read Luther without encountering again and again the ironic moves that break up continuities and systems of correspondence, but a total surrender of analogy would lead to cynicism, even nihilism.

The relationship is "asymmetrical" in that what appears to be the case in one set of categories that belong to one of the régimes (spiritual or earthly) is not simply reflected in the other, but is shaped by it in unexpected ways. Luther moves constantly between the audible and the visible to articulate this issue of relating the Word to the mask (or the world) and vice versa; this allows him to keep alive his ironic destabilizing tone and not succumb to the dominant analogical method. He keeps searching for correspondences, however, for that is what the metaphor of the mask conveys; it is itself an analogical move. Luther's theology is neither a total synthesis nor a complete separation, yet simultaneously it is both; it is irony breaking into the realm of analogy. What the mask reveals is the very Word hidden in its cracks.

---

[20] Martin Luther, "Heidelberg Disputation (1518)," *Luther's Works* vol. 31 *Career of the Reformer I*, ed. and trans. Harold J. Grimm (Philadelphia: Fortress Press, 1957), 39–70; *WA* 1:353–74.

Irony, to convey something by using concepts, ideas, and words that suggest the opposite of their literal meaning, and not analogy, is what Luther aims at by defining the cross as revelation under its opposite (*revelatio sub contraria specie*). Analogy functions by the rule of correspondence, which allows one to know the unknown by the known. In theology two analogies have been dominant to establish the relationship between God and the created world: correspondences of attributes (we know who God is because we are God's creatures: *analogia attributionis*) or of proportions (God is related to the divine's own being as creatures are to their being: *analogia proportionalitatis*). The *suum cuique* when applied to our relation to God relies totally on analogy. It defines God's infinite justice by inferring from our finite standards of justice and establishes God's relation to the Son based on our own relations with others. When we apply this theological use of analogy to the question of justice the result is conveyed by an old Latin expression that Luther was fond of quoting, the "heathen Terence"—*summum ius summa iniuria* ("the strictest law is the greatest injustice").[21]

When he answered thus and placed his "new definition" against the classic definition of justice, Luther was employing irony to subvert the established canons of jurisprudence, and of rationality in general. The distinction he drew between reason and faith was a departure from the scholastic consensus that made reason an infrastructure for faith; the latter fulfilled the former (*donum superadditum*), bringing it to perfection by means of analogy. Luther's gesture was an ironic deconstruction of analogy: that which seems to be is in fact its opposite.

Faith and Reason

Luther's irony suggests a dialectical relation in which faith engages reason but presses it to its limits, to the margins of its validity, to the point where it no longer works and has to be abandoned for what he calls faith, and not brought to perfection by faith. If the concept of Christ as the new

---

[21] Martin Luther, "Whether Soldiers, Too, Can Be Saved (1526)," *Luther's Works* vol. 46 *Christian in Society III*, ed. and rev. Robert C. Schultz, trans, Charles M. Jacobs (Philadelphia: Fortress Press, 1967), 100; *WA* 19, 630, 3.

justice had to be "understood," it had to be understood paradoxically, not accommodated in the established canons of rationality. Theology, *qua theologia crucis*, cannot stay inside the recognized forms of discourse. Luther's approach to language itself, his contempt for the Ciceronian Latin of his days (the official language of theology), further exemplifies this attitude.[22] This faith that the Reformer calls radical trust (*fiducia*) is characterized by trust in and fear of the Word of God, the truth, always breaking through human words, rendering human theological constructions invalid, going against the grain of the dominant systems, the rules of the familiar, the law of the house (*oeconomia*).

Oswald Bayer, commenting on a letter Luther wrote to Melanchthon in 1530, said, "the truth of faith is not communicable as a merchandise."[23] It falls outside the normal rules by which the régimes of truth operate in philosophy, politics, economy, and in the church.

What were those "economies," those rules and norms by which the "house" was ordered and given a rationale? The dominant model for church and theology in Luther's time was the so-called *via antiqua*, represented by the theology of Thomas Aquinas, which supposed a rationale ingeniously construed around the atonement theory of Anselm (discussed above). In God's economy, the analogy was conceived in terms of the prevailing mercantilism of the age, a payment in the form of a punishment is devised in order to satisfy God's wrath by a vicarious substitution. God sends the Son who, through the incarnation, becomes truly human, except for sin, and can vicariously offer the fair payment that satisfies the requirements of justice. How are we to cash in this payment? We only need to do what is in us (*facere quod in se est*—to do what is in one) and because of Christ's sacrifice we no longer are required to do what we cannot. This is sufficient, for God has created us with the capability of doing that much, and doing that much is necessary so we might gain the deal already accomplished. The formula is similar to a matching fund: if we come up with our part,

---

[22] See Vítor Westhelle, "Communication and the Transgression of Language in Martin Luther," *Lutheran Quarterly* XVII, no. 1 (Spring 2003): 1–27.

[23] Cited by Oswald Bayer, *Gott als Autor: Zur einen poietologischen Theologie* (Tübingen: Mohr Siebeck, 1999), 260.

which we can and should, Christ pays the rest—a totally reasonable argument, congruent with the rules of the economy and jurisprudence at the time.

This economic-juridical model is shaken precisely at the time in history when a credit system was born and the first monetary denominations were issued. Unlike gold or a precious coin, these units had no any intrinsic value in themselves but were guaranteed a stipulated nominal value by the ruler or by a bank. This phenomenon is at the origin of the early capitalist financial system in the thirteenth and fourteenth centuries; it insinuated itself into the very rationality of theological reasoning. The new theological construction, called *via moderna*, elevated the importance of the ruler or the bank to control and warrant the economic process instead of leaving it to direct market exchange. In theology this led to the *pactum*-theology, the contract-theology which argued that humans' merits had only negligible intrinsic value (like paper money) but they could be cashed at the value guaranteed by God, the banker/ ruler.

The early Luther found this an appealing correction to the former model. It would grant more autonomy to God in the process of justification and would diminish to a negligible amount what is in us. God would do much more and yet not all. And in the fluctuating monetary market, how was this negligible value, which was still necessary, to be determined? This question was one reason that even this model would be challenged in Luther's later formulation of the theology of the cross. A strict analogical argument still ruled, as the example above clearly shows.[24] Only the terms of the correspondence changed, because human experience changed with the societal transformations produced by the emerging economic system of financial capitalism.

What marks the rediscovery of the theology of the cross in this context is the attempt to free theology from the captivity of the dominant modes of rationality, which not by coincidence were in sync with dominant jurisprudence and economic reasoning. In other words, the scandal of the

---

[24] The simile of the monetary system comes from Ockham and was of public domain at the time of the Reformation. See McGrath, *Luther's Theology of the Cross*, 59.

cross can only be maintained if it also remains as a scandal, like a thorn, to our statutes of reason, no matter what canonic or confessional form they take.

Hence it is not a coincidence that two issues that gave the early contour to the Reformation movement were at the very core of this economic rationality: usury and indulgences. The Heidelberg Disputation reflects everywhere a struggle with the language of the two dominant and related fields of economy and jurisprudence; it is the problem of *work* (regimented by economics) and of the *law* (regimented by jurisprudence). These are the régimes Luther sets against the word of the cross. In the Heidelberg Disputation the argument starts in the first thesis with opposition between the "law of God" (God's "jurisprudence") and human righteousness (human understanding of justice). From the second thesis onward Luther draws the same sharp distinction between the work of God (the divine "economy") and human work (human economy). At thesis 20 he says a theologian can only deserve to be called a theologian if theology is done from the standpoint of suffering and the cross. What would be the alternative? Theology based on what reason is able to rationalize, what jurisprudence is able to justify, and what the market is able to regulate regarding the value of labor.

By bringing up the cross and suffering, Luther suggests that a theologian be guided by what the canons of rationality consider foolishness and not wisdom (theses 22, 24, 30). When Luther uses the words *cross* (used simultaneously for both the literal and metaphorical meaning), *suffering*, and *death* interchangeably, it can be seen as signaling the point where the conventional semantic meaning of a rational discourse breaks down. Hence, if the experiences of suffering, cross, and death are the reference for theology, they are in themselves the experience of a deficit that the economy cannot balance within the rules of its trade. Only grace (*charis, gratia*, gift) can therefore provide the answer. The gift as grace subverts the economic order. To accept the gift is not even an action, it requires a passive (and passionate, therefore) relinquishment of any reliance on the rules of the trade. Any attempt to return the gift or pay for it even minimally destroys it. This is what Luther decries when he talks about using the best in the worst manner (thesis 24).

Jürgen Moltmann comments that the theology of the cross defies the epistemological principle of Western metaphysics by which the similar knows the similar. His substitute resembles the Hippocratic allopathic principle in medicine by which cures come from producing effects that are opposed to those of the organisms they attack (*contraria contrariis curantur*).[25] It also points to the break of analogy as the epistemological principle of theology.[26] A theology of the cross has, as it were, an allopathic principle at its core; a poison is at the same time a medicine (both denoted by the same Greek term *pharmakon*). It is in the face of death that life is a gift; it is in the face of the cross that resurrection is a word of grace; it is in suffering that salvation (health) is freely received. Irony appears again. Against analogy (the resemblance of some particulars otherwise unknown) we have the unsettling graceful, but not superfluous, intervention of irony.

To clarify Luther's claims, one simply should read the Heidelberg Disputation backwards, from the last theses on philosophy to the first ones on theology. This curious experiment applies to the reading of the text the reversal of the same ironic version embedded in its organization. The irony is this: contrary to the Scholastic practice of starting with philosophical axioms to support the theological assertions that follow, the Disputation concludes with philosophical theses as if they were an afterthought, a mere supplement. Not much attention has been given to those theses in Luther research. He did not add explanatory commentaries, as he did for all his theological theses.

The experiment of reading the theses backwards, thus following the normal order of a Scholastic structure, produces an interesting result. Consider theses 29-30: "He who wishes to philosophize by using Aristotle without danger to his soul must first become thoroughly foolish in Christ. Just as a person does not use the evil of passion well unless he is a married man, so no person philosophizes well unless he is a fool, that is a Christian." Luther's remaining ten theses scold Aristotle

---

[25] Moltmann, *Crucified God*, 27.
[26] This is a point that had been made by the early Karl Barth in his criticism of *analogia entis*. See his "Schicksal und Idee in der Theologie," *Zwischen den Zeiten* 7 (1929), 309–48.

directly or indirectly. In fact, they are not "philosophical" theses in the traditional sense. They are a gesture of ironic contempt against the highest foundational standard of rationality and the propaedeutic (preliminary course) for all theological work.

Aristotle was the philosopher who provided the groundwork for the "received view" of the Middle Ages. He was also the indisputable yardstick of Scholastic theology. A year earlier in the "Disputation against Scholastic Theology" (theses 43-44 and 50) Luther said: "It is an error to say that no man can become a theologian without Aristotle. Indeed, no one can become a theologian unless he becomes one without Aristotle. Briefly, the whole of Aristotle is to theology as darkness is to light. This in opposition to the scholastics." Luther lectured on Aristotle's *Nicomachean Ethics* in his early years at Wittenberg, but since those lectures were lost very little can be said with certainty about his knowledge of the Greek philosopher. Aristotle was the very measure and standard for most of theology that Luther despised; that much is known and is sufficient to explain his rage against the Greek philosopher.

Luther insists that theology should work in a context of faith. This reading of the Heidelberg Disputation from back to front suggests a plausible hypothesis that the name Aristotle stood for what the Reformer regarded as the dominant mode of reasoning, really any mode of reasoning that would norm the theological discourse apart from faith. The philosopher's very name functioned as a metonymy! That means his name stands for the hegemonic or prevailing philosophy that at that time informed theology. Martin Heidegger was probably the first in modern times to recognize in Luther's theology, most incisively represented by the Heidelberg Disputation, an epistemological gesture that first deconstructed the Western philosophical tradition known as ontotheology, which relies on the definition of God as Being constructed in analogy to beings. In 1927, at the awakening of the Luther renaissance, Heidegger wrote in *Being and Time*:

Theology is seeking a more primordial interpretation of man's Being toward God, prescribed by the meaning of faith itself and remaining within it. It is slowly beginning to understand once more Luther's insight that the 'foundation' on which its system of dogma rests has not arisen from an enquiry in which faith is primary, and that conceptually this 'foundation' not only is inadequate for the problematic of theology, but conceals and distorts it.[27]

Luther was not proposing another mode of rationality to substitute for Aristotle's, however. He could praise Aristotle as he did as late as 1540 in his "Admonition to Pastors to Preach against Usury."[28] His point was that as far as theology is concerned, as opposed to jurisprudence, politics, or economics, Aristotle could not be the norm. The distinction between the earthly and the spiritual régimes requires different semantic realms. "All words are made new when they are transferred from their context to a different one…as we raise [our voice] to heaven, in face of God our speech is a new language," said Luther on the distinctiveness of discourse in theology.[29] This language is closer to poetry than philosophy; it invests more in rhetoric than in logic, as Luther has often suggested.[30] In the words of Oswald Bayer,

> The Aristotelian understanding of justice pertains to the political forum and should not be scolded; here it is valid. However to scold and reject decisively is the transposition of this understanding to the theological forum. Luther sticks to the distinction by which language has two semantic realms, one is properly theological and the other political: *Duplex est forum, theologicum et politicum.*[31]

---

[27] Martin Heidegger, *Being and Time* (New York: Harper & Row, 1962), 30; see also *Aussprache mit Martin Heidegger an 06/XI/1951* in *Seminare, G.A.* (Frankfurt: Suhrkamp, 1986), 436–37; further references to Luther by Heidegger to this effect and with a commentary are offered by Jean-Luc Marion, *God without Being* (Chicago: University of Chicago Press, 1991), 61–73.

[28] *WA* 51, 331–424.

[29] *Omnia vocabula fiunt nova, quando e su foro in alienum transferuntur. … Cum ascendimus coelum, coram Deo loquendum nobis est novis linguis. WA* 39/I, 231, 1–3, 14–16.

[30] See Bayer, *Gott als Autor*, 278–79.

[31] Ibid., 290–91.

The distinction pertains to whether one is speaking *coram mundo* or *coram deo*—in face of the world or in face of God. The double forum corresponds to the double knowledge of God. In face of the world (*coram mundo*) analogy works, but only to the point where irony intervenes to move us, to make us change our minds and convert to the other perspective, or to the perspective of the Other (*coram deo*).

What the eyes cannot see, faith brings to vision. The theology of the cross is the radical affirmation that faith is only possible when the evidences that point directly and unambiguously to the divine are not there, when analogy no longer rules, when all we see is the back side of God (*posteriora dei*) or God's rear end, as Luther translated Exodus 33:23.[32] It is not that goodness and beauty do not tell us anything. Luther explicitly recognized a *duplex cognitio dei* (a double knowledge of God).[33] Luther allows for some analogical arguments,[34] as he allows Aristotle's mode of reasoning a proper place in philosophy and politics. Indeed, out of the goodness of God's creation we can be instructed in God's will toward us. Even the fields and the trees can be sermons better than most preached in churches, Luther said.[35] But this knowledge is only of an exemplary character. It is only right and proper for us to follow this path once we have been led in the right direction; once we have already been turned around, converted (*metanoia*) from the old ways of the world and its reasoning to another way.

Luther's ironic gesture, in this sense an apocalyptic move, is carried also into the semantic field. All apocalyptic literature evokes images that bring us to the limits of what we can imagine; Luther's exploration of the possibilities of theology drove him in the same direction, although

---

[32] "Und wenn ich meine Hand von dir thue, wirst du mir hinten nachsehen; aber mein Angesicht kann man nicht sehen."

[33] Martin Luther, *Luther's Works* vol. 26 *Lectures on Galatians (1535) Chapters 1–4*, ed. and trans. Jaroslav Pelikan (St. Louis: Concordia, 1963), 399–400. See Vítor Westhelle, "Cross, Creation, and Ecology: The Meeting Point between the Theology of the Cross and Creation Theology in Luther," in *Concern for Creation: Voices on the Theology of Creation*, ed. Viggo Mortensen (Uppsala: Tro & Tanke, 1995), 159–68.

[34] This is what is not recognized in the work of McGrath, *Luther's Theology of the Cross*, or in Gerhard Forde, *On Being a Theologian of the Cross* (Grand Rapids: Eerdmans, 1997)

[35] *WA* 42, 156, 24–26.

everything in him did not echo the apocalyptic tonality. He was a very earthly person, so earthly that he was not ashamed of it.[36] He could call reason a whore and also say it is "the best of all, indeed something divine."[37] What reason was not allowed was the right to speculate about God or to norm God's Word. There he drew the line and sounded the apocalyptic tone. Theology of the cross—*Theologia crucis*—became the shorthand for this apocalyptic move. Theology of glory—*Theologia gloriae*—in turn, was to surrender theology to the canons of rationality prevalent in the juridical, political, economic, and ecclesial world.

Cross and the Apocalyptic

For Luther, the theology of the cross is above all a practice, a way of doing theology, a disposition of theologizing according to the cross (*kata stauron*). *Theologia crucis* is about speaking a risky and dissonant word, a word that cannot be cashed into the system, that does not fit into the economy, the rules of this earthly house; in short, it is not a merchandise. The Greeks called this form of speaking *parrhesia*, the act of speaking boldly, plainly, for the sake of the truth itself that might cost everything, including one's own life. The *parrhesiast* does not hold anything back, as in saving an argument for strategic reasons, or in concealing some knowledge only to be used as a last resort. *Parrhesia* is always a last word, an apocalyptic word. That is actually what the Heidelberg Disputation declares: "the theologian of the cross calls the thing what it is" (thesis 21). And this naming of things is for the Reformer a way of avoiding speculation. It is a way of stopping at the point where reason wants to take over and explain faith away. Worth noting is that Luther most often speaks about the theologian of the cross, and not of the theology of the cross; it is theology in the making and not an objective treatise, a systematic compendium; it is from the standpoint of the cross that theology is done. In a sermon of 1525 he sharply distinguishes the "discourse about passion" from the "practice of passion" (*praedicare passionis Christi et usus passionis*), saying that the devil

---

[36] Agnes Heller, *Renaissance Man* (New York: Schocken, 1978), 203–04.

[37] *Ratio omniumrerum res et caput et prae caeteris rebus huis vitae optimum et divinum quiddam sit.* WA 39/I, 175, 9–10.

is he who does the former.[38] His argument is almost like Job's against his friends. If it comes to it, it is better to blame God, this hidden and ineffable God (*deus absconditus*), than to try to account for God's ways, to justify God. In this sense, the theology of the cross is a radical rejection of theodicy or even its reversal. God does our justifying; we don't justify God. We cannot explain the invisible through the visible, the unknown through the known, as analogy believes possible.

If Christian theology, as *theologia crucis*, lies in its practice (*usus*) and not in its preaching or theory, it is because it is not a theology based primarily on an epiphany, on a magnificent unambiguous revelation of God. Even what we call "epiphany" in the church calendar is the celebration of a manifestation of the divine in a barn, with animals, flies, and manure. Epiphany is not an unequivocal manifestation of the divinity; it is indirect and even expressed in its reverse: glory lies in a manger, power in fragility, wisdom in foolishness.

Even what has just been said can be a dangerous argument, however, when it turns itself once more into a speculative strategy about God's ways of dispensing salvation, as when Luther himself suggests that God breaks down in order to restore.[39] His way of expressing his theological convictions was never totally free from his monastic practices and techniques of acquiring spiritual humility that so much shaped his early life. Nevertheless, he himself was aware of this danger as he distinguished between two senses of humility or humbleness.[40] One describes a state of affairs. The other is a technique of the self to make oneself pleasing to God, leading one to seek humility. Luther in hindsight claimed that in his monastic years he was the best at humility. Hence, when he talks about God "breaking down in order to restore," the meaning intended is not to describe God's economy of salvation and prescribe our moral duty, but to prevent us from saying that we accomplish the merit of salvation by our "works," even those of humility. God saves us when we are at a stage of humbleness, brokenness, and depravity because that is when God reaches

---

[38] *WA* 17/I, 71, 26–28.

[39] Regin Prenter, *Luther's Theology of the Cross* (Philadelphia: Fortress Press, 1971), 15–17.

[40] See McGrath, *Luther's Theology of the Cross*, 117–28.

us; and not because we have made our way down there, but rather because we are no longer in denial over our condition. We might use the example of Mary, which Luther finds paradigmatic to describe this theological attitude. Was it God who put down Mary only to lift her up? No! The point is that God raised her from exactly that state of lowness where she stood and confessed herself to be. Humility is not a technique to get God's grace, it is not a merchandise to be exchanged for grace; it is rather the admission of one's wretchedness; it is about being plain and honest to ourselves and the world by naming things for what they are.

In an insightful article, Lutheran theologian Timothy Wengert has shown that what Luther called the "alien work of God" (*opus alienum*) is not a prescriptive statement but purely descriptive; it says that this is what our condition and our experience of it is. The rest is speculation.[41] It seems as if God has abandoned us. Those who recognize this are no longer resisting God's grace; nevertheless revolt and lament is not to be shunned. Using present-day terminology, God's preferential option for the poor, the outcast, those suffering devastating illness is a redundancy to the extent that these are the people who by knowing themselves as such, and insofar as they do, are ready to count on God's grace to lift them up, as God has done with that lowly unwed and pregnant maid from Galilee.

But can we totally avoid a mysterious and even sinister aspect of the divine in the face of the inexplicable suffering of the innocent victim? As Brian Gerrish[42] has pointed out, following Walther von Löwenich and Paul Althaus before him, there is ambivalence in Luther's understanding of God's hiddenness, which can be expressed in two different senses of hiddenness, a hiddenness *in* and a hiddenness *behind* the cross. These distinct senses of hiddenness, in turn, run parallel to two ways of understanding God's *opus alienum*. In the words of Alistair McGrath, "Indeed,

---

[41] Timothy Wengert, "'Peace, Peace…Cross, Cross': Reflections on How Martin Luther Relates the Theology of the Cross to Suffering," *Theology Today* 59, no. 2 (July 2002): 190–205, particularly 200.

[42] Brian A. Gerrish, "'To the Unknown God': Luther and Calvin on the Hiddenness of God," *Journal of Religion* 53, no. 3 (July 1973): 263–92. See also McGrath, *Luther's Theology of the Cross*, 164–65, and David Tracy, "The Hidden God: The Divine Other of Liberation," *Cross Currents* 46, no. 1 (Spring 1996): 5–16.

there are excellent reasons for suggesting that Luther uses the term *Deus absconditus* in two main senses, which have little in common apart from the general idea of 'hiddenness'."[43] If God is hidden *in* the cross, then God partakes in the passion of Christ. If God is hidden behind the cross so that the divine immutability, majesty, and power are only veiled and not affected by the cross, however, then God's mystery is not revealed in the cross, not even under its opposite. The consequence of such an interpretation would lead us into the bosom of a mysterious and terrifying God. But if God were in that cross, we would have the notion of a God whose compassion reached such depth. The temptation is clearly to opt for "in" and shun "behind." But are these really exclusive options? Should we not recognize in God both the *fascinans* and the *tremendum*, as Rudolf Otto summarized the attributes of the holy?

This double sense to be found in Luther does not represent alternative options for interpretation. Both are valid and one does not exclude the other. God's hidden work is a way of naming in a radical way our experience of being abandoned by God as Jesus himself experienced. In the Eastern Orthodox tradition, Gregory Nazianzen could speak even of an uproar, dissention, uprising (*stasis*) within the Trinity itself.[44] This is the reason for the biblical tradition of lament and even revolt in the midst of faith itself as a hard but a necessary stance to take if we want to avoid the other options. One of these options is to attribute to human sin such power that it can defy and cancel out God's grace. This is the position of Job's "theological" friends that have since given theology a bad reputation. The second is to attribute evil to an ontic agent, the devil as a hypostasis, which would imply Manichaeism and would compromise monotheism. The third would be to abandon faith and surrender to nihilism. If these are not to be followed, how do we reconcile these divergent senses of hiddenness?

---

[43] McGrath, *Luther's Theology of the Cross*, 164–65.
[44] Gregory Nazianzen, "The Third Theological Oration," II, in *Nicene and Post-Nicene Fathers* (Peabody, Mass.: Hendrickson, 1995), 7:301.

In an illuminating paper, David Tracy has these pertinent comments to offer on the double sense of hiddenness:

> The central dilemma for Christian self-understanding is that Luther *does* speak…of a second sense of hiddenness. He even dares to speak of a second sense of hiddenness as behind or even 'beyond' the word. At the very least, this literally awful, ambivalent sense of God's hiddenness can be so overwhelming that God is sometimes experienced as purely frightening, not tender, sometimes even as an impersonal reality—"it"— of sheer power and energy signified by such metaphors, such *fragmentary* metaphors as abyss, chasm, chaos, horror….This Hiddenness allows for a new theological recovery of apocalyptic as a fragmenting form in our own period. Indeed, to 'let God be God again' is also to let that awesome and numinous strand of our common Christian heritage be heard again with the kind of clarity and courage that Luther found in his apocalyptic visions of history and nature alike, and, in his willingness to dare to speak of God's hiddenness in the full sense.[45]

In his argument against Erasmus in the "Bondage of the Will," Luther, in defending the clarity of the Scriptures (*claritatis scripturae*), says that whatever is not revealed in it belongs to a mystery that we cannot explain or dare to speculate about; the Scriptures are enough (*sola scriptura*).[46] Unlike Calvin, he refuses to venture into the territory that explores God's intent or election. This territory remains uncharted. But it is better to admit that there is an inscrutable shadow-side to God than the other options available to us. It would be simply a descriptive statement of our finite experience, and of the very finitude of our reason. But if it is blasphemy, it is the one of Job. This is the one God is great enough to take.

A moving description of such apostasy is rendered by Shusaku Endo's novel *Silence*, in which a Christian under torture for his faith is demanded

---

[45] Center for Theological Inquiry, David Tracy, *Form and Fragment* (22 March 2002); available online at www.Ctinquiry.org/publications/reflections_volume_3/tracy.htm (accessed 5 July 2006). The same argument was developed earlier by the author in "The Hidden God," *Cross Currents* 46/1 (Spring 1996): 5–16.

[46] Martin Luther, "The Bondage of the Will," *Luther's Works* vol. 33 *Career of the Reformer III*, ed. and trans. Philip S. Watson (Philadelphia: Fortress Press, 1972), 60.

to trample over an image of Christ to save not only himself but other Christians, whose cries he could hear in the dungeons, and who would continue to be tortured unless he committed apostasy. Upon the prisoner's refusal and the resulting unabated torture of his follow prisoners, Christ spoke to him from that image: "Trample on, trample on; this is why I came." Mercy and wrath, grace and condemnation are in an epidermic relationship; they rub each other skin to skin.

Luther in Context

A suggestive hypothesis for framing the Reformer's ambivalent rendition of hiddenness is that Luther's context was so ridden with social injustices that it could not be accommodated with the sense of hiddenness *in*. There were realities that, to use Tracy's expression, were behind the cross and behind and beyond the Word.

Until recently not much attention has been given to how the social conditions under which Luther lived were determinant for his theology. How contextual was Luther's theology? It is difficult to imagine that Luther's use of the cross in both the historical or literal and metaphorical meanings simultaneously, and his "essential identification"[47] between the cross and human suffering in general could be affirmed without a close awareness of the social and economic conditions of his time and place. Would he be talking about suffering without being aware of the plague epidemics rampant at the time? Was he not aware of the fact that the commerce of indulgences that brought economic burden to the poor was flourishing precisely because so many would die without the assistance of priests and relatives and thus be condemned to purgatory? Were they not kept away from contact with the general population in order to prevent further spreading of the disease and thus denied access to the last rites? Didn't his sermons and treaties on usury show a sophisticated awareness of the virulent practice of the emerging financial capitalism that led Marx to call him "the first German political economist"? And was he also not aware

---

[47] See Regin Prenter, "Zur Theologie des Kreuzes bei Luther," *Lutherische Rundschau* 3 (November 1959), 279.

of the marginal position of Germany Saxony in the Empire, as he often complained about the poor and wretched state of German territories?

The challenge for us is to be able to discern, as Luther did, the places and times in which brokenness, the damaged life, the deep cutting crises are receiving a facelift from the high priests of the new global gospel, what the Canadian theologian Douglas John Hall calls the cult of "official optimism." From this standpoint one can understand also what the dangers are in what Hall dubbed as "resurrectionism," which implies the cross as being only a transitional and disposable stage that can be left to oblivion after we have climbed to the glory of Easter. One has to be constantly reminded of the fact that the resurrected body carries with it the scars of the cross. We shall be dealing with the resurrection at a greater length later, but suffice it here to say that the resurrection accounts should not be read as leaving behind the passion of Christ in the shadow of his glorious victory. It ought to be read as an affirmation, and not an overcoming, of the fact that in that moment of absence and darkness God was indeed present. One could say that if the passion and cross of Jesus is the subtext of all Christian theology, the resurrection functions as a meta-text, something like a commentary at the margin of the text used to make sure that its meaning is elucidated at least for the reader who entered the comments. But it does not override or erase the main text. This "meta-text" can never undo the scandal of the grounding narrative, lest we miss the whole point.

Here we have an invitation to face with hope, but a hope against all hope, the terrible void, the *horror vacui* of a God that, according to our perception, cannot be but the One who is against God. In Luther's words: *ad deum contra deum confungere*, "to flee from and find refuge in God against God."[48] Such is the impossibility that makes theology possible.

---

[48] *WA* 5, 204, 26f.

Uses and Abuses
Modern Critiques and Responses

4

Christianity's stroke of genius: God sacrificing himself for the guilt of humans.

Friedrich Nietzsche

The cross is often viewed and criticized as an expression of defeatism, or a paralyzing cult of suffering (dolorism), or an atoning event that accomplished spiritual deliverance but is not connected with present suffering. The words of Antonio Machado resound as an enduring indictment: "I don't want and will not sing to this Jesus of the tree, but to the one who walked on the sea."[1] Evasions of the cross with its crude scandalous brutality were not uncommon, beginning in the early days of the Christian faith. Some found reassurance in the life of Jesus' radical love ethic in which the cross figures as a tragic event, which might, at best, symbolically reiterate the breadth and length and height and depth of this love, as Ephesians 3:18 eloquently renders it. Others found solace in the resurrection accounts that shadowed the cross scandal into the dim background; the resurrection would then project itself victoriously in fine, bright resolution.

---

[1] Antonio Machado, *Poesías* (Buenos Aires: Losada, 1977), 150.

In spite of these attractive alternatives, rejections of the embarrassment of the event that Paul called scandalous and foolish (1 Cor. 1:23), most early Christians remained steadfast, keeping the cross central. As we have discussed, however, since the fourth century we have another mode of evasion: the cross was no longer a symbol of derision in Christian piety; instead it represented a sublime, haughty triumph. The Reformation was the moment when this mechanism of sublimation was exposed. And every time it is exposed the spirit of the Reformation becomes alive.

After the historical Reformation of the sixteenth century, a sea change took place: the Enlightenment. In its philosophical and theological dimensions, the German Enlightenment, in particular, brought about a challenge to three axiomatic claims that even opponents of Christianity had until then not seriously challenged. They were known as the three "historical proofs" of Christianity. First was the belief that Jesus Christ was the fulfillment of the Old Testament prophecies. The second proof was the historical reliability of the accounts of miracles in the Christian Testament, including the resurrection of Jesus. The third, less significant for use as a proof case, was the expansion of Christianity. The secularizing impact of the Enlightenment and the subsequent historical recognition of the far more impressive expansion of the younger Islamic faith, in addition to the impermeability of Eastern religions to missionary efforts, buried this argument early. But the first two "proofs" stood unchallenged through the eighteenth century.

Even early opponents of Christianity such as Celsus or Porphyry would not question the supernatural claims Christians made about their miracle stories, only their claim to exclusivity. In the eighteenth century the philological works of Reimarus on the Old Testament (published later by G. E. Lessing) opened the tight-sealed lid of this truism. And Lessing's famous claim that, as far as establishing their rational validity, there is an "abject, broad ditch" (*garstige breite Graben*) between us and those events resounds to this day in all modern scholarship as normative: "accidental truths of history can never become the proof of necessary truths of reason."[2]

---

[2] G. E. Lessing, "On the Proof of the Spirit and of Power," in *Lessing's Theological Writings*, ed. Henry Chadwick (Stanford: Stanford University Press, 1956), 53.

The Enlightenment's changes in the patterns of the régime of truth brought fundamental changes in the assessment of Jesus' crucifixion. The implications of these changes are logically foreseeable from the collapse of the so-called historical proofs of Christianity. First, if it is untenable to hold Jesus to be the fulfillment of the Old Testament, then the crucifixion accounts are reduced to the story of the tragic death of a charismatic prophet. Second, if the miracle stories are on shaky ground because they cannot be verified historically, so would be the resurrection accounts. The result is that the passion and crucifixion of Jesus are bracketed, disconnected from the life of Jesus and from the resurrection. This raises suspicion that Christianity is a religion mesmerized by the passion narrative, with the miracles and the resurrection simply adornments employed to sublimate the cross and suffering, or shields to protect the passion narrative from being turned into shoddy tragedy. Two main criticisms have afflicted modern theology in its attempt to address the crucifixion. One comes from the Enlightenment and is represented by Lessing; the other is typified by Friedrich Nietzsche.

The Enlightenment and the Tragic-Death Criticism

The first critique comes from the early Enlightenment as represented by Lessing and, in a less sardonic tone, by Immanuel Kant. The argument is that focus on the suffering and cross of Christ, adorned with miracle accounts, led to a denial of the God of love and compassion; such love and compassion are not found in the crucifixion accounts but in the teachings of Jesus. Lessing suggests that an inversion took place. Miracle stories and the fulfillment of Old Testament prophecies were emphasized to boost the importance of Jesus' teachings, but they were received as the core of the narrative, displacing the focus from the center of the picture to its adornments on the periphery. This is Lessing's argument:

> I deny that they [miracles and fulfillment of prophesies] can and should bind me to the very least faith in the other teachings of Christ. What then does bind me? Nothing but these teachings themselves. Eighteen hundred years ago they were so new, so alien, so foreign to the entire

mass of truths recognized at that age, that nothing less than miracles and fulfilled prophecies were required if the multitude were to attend to them at all.[3]

And what were these teachings? In another text Lessing tells with delight an apocryphal story, attributed to St. Jerome, about John the Evangelist. Legend has it that John regularly delivered the homily at his congregation. But as he got older he grew infirm and finally had to be carried to the church. His sermons grew shorter every time he preached, until one day he only said, "Little children, love one another." In the following weeks John recovered his strength, but while delivering the homily he continued to say only, "Little children, love one another." His disciples thought the brevity of his orations was due to his frail condition. John enlightened them: because it is the Lord's command and this alone, when done, is sufficient.[4]

Before Ludwig Feuerbach said, "If God is love, then love is God," Lessing had suggested it. All the dogmas of the church are an impediment to the practice of love, including the doctrines of atonement. Remembering Anselm's theory in particular, Lessing and his followers maintained that it presents a God whose compassion has to be subjugated to juridical principles of justice and is thus bound to combine judgment with mercy. Ultimately this theory deprives humans of authentic freedom to practice love unencumbered by questions of divine justice. And Lessing concludes with a rhetorical question: "Which of the two is the more difficult? To accept and confess the Christian dogmas, or to practice Christian love?"[5]

It is interesting that this criticism was anticipated in Peter's rebuttal of Jesus' announcement of his passion in Mark 8. Peter could not understand that the one who was compassionate and obedient to God would not be spared so that his message could be spread. The outbreak of hatred at the end could not be the result of lifelong practice and teaching of love. Such an end would mean that the *Abba* Jesus professed would betray true fatherly love in the end. The passage begins with Peter's confession: "You

[3] Ibid., 55.

[4] "The Testament of John," in ibid., 57–61.

[5] Ibid., p. 60.

are the Christ." Immediately afterward Jesus foretells his coming suffering, to which Peter objects and receives the rebuke of Jesus: "Get behind me, Satan!"

The evangelist inserts this confession at the very center of his Gospel account, when the focus turns to Jesus' passion. This passion narrative starts with Peter's "true" confession and ends with the death of Jesus in chapter 15. It is immediately followed by the centurion's unlikely and astonishing confession: "Truly this man was the son of God" (Mark 15:39). The confession of the centurion, which closes the passion narrative in Mark, proves to be the true one. Peter's confession is empty for he does not accept that the fate of the Messiah is passion. This organization of the narrative seems intended. While Peter was close to Jesus and his teachings, the Roman officer—who knew little of Jesus, probably only that he had just breathed his last on the cross—was the witness whose confession was validated by the evangelist.

Unlike Mark's Gospel, the Enlightenment, by severing the historical accounts that pointed to the proofs of Christianity (miracle stories and fulfillment of prophecy) from that which reason can demonstrate, left the cross behind as a historical event without redemption, a tragic but meaningless death among legions of other executions. The resurrection, improbable according to reason, did not do the trick and reclaim that death. What was left could only be sustained on other grounds, the reasonable moral values of the teachings of Jesus. These teachings were all that survived that tragedy. The cross was seen only as an appalling event, the tragic end of someone who lived love all the way to the last consequences.

For those who remained behind, the teaching was the thing that had to be kept: we know God not from the one hanging there on the cross, but by the example of love shown through his life and teachings. What results is a theology of the Word (as moral teachings) without the cross, which fostered a renewal of the story of Jesus' teachings but no longer needed the cross to anchor it. It would have made no difference if Jesus had died in bed of old age.

The Enlightenment disparaged the necessity of the cross in the divine economy. The moral example (Jesus?) can be reasonably defended, not a sacrificial atonement, not even an inevitable fateful outcome of the life Jesus lived. The revelation of God would not be what Paul called the apocalypse of Jesus Christ and him crucified, but the moral education of humanity. As Lessing would say in his lapidary motto: "Education is revelation coming to the individual; and revelation is education which has come, and is still coming, to the human race."[6] The cross does not attest to or corroborate Jesus' teachings about a loving God. If the cross cannot be redeemed it cannot have any redemptive meaning either. Any emphasis laid on the cross betrays the message of love for which Jesus lived.

When Albert Schweitzer closed his studies on the nineteenth-century quest for the historical Jesus, and before he left theology for medicine and went to Africa, he gave proper expression to this sense of frustration with which a life of love ironically ended:

> In the knowledge that he is the coming Son of Man He [Jesus] lays hold of the wheel of the world to set it moving on that last revolution which is to bring our ordinary history to a close. It refuses to turn, and He throws himself upon it. Then it does turn; and crushes Him. Instead of bringing in the eschatological conditions, He has destroyed them. The wheel rolls onward, and the mangled body of the immeasurably great Man, who was strong enough to think of Himself as the spiritual ruler of mankind and to bend history to His purpose, is hanging on it still. That is His victory and His reign.[7]

Such criticism resounds throughout nineteenth-century liberal theology, of which Schweitzer is the final expression and the first departure, and has found its way into some more recent liberation and feminist theologies. To these the cross would only attest to the absence or impossibility of what the world most needs: a God of love and of justice for the downtrodden. C. S. Song has called for theology to move "toward the day when the cross…will be abolished." And in the meantime, he continues, "Christian mission is shaped by what Jesus said and did during

6 "The Education of the Human Race," in ibid., 83.
7 Albert Schweitzer, *The Quest of the Historical Jesus: A Critical Study of Its Progress from Reimarus to Wrede* (New York: Macmillan, 1968), 370–71.

his life and ministry."[8] Joanne Carlson Brown and Rebecca Parker argue that the "travesty of the suffering and the death of Jesus is not redeemed by the resurrection....Suffering is never redemptive, and suffering cannot be redeemed. The cross is a sign of tragedy."[9] Others, in a more moderate tone, ask for a moratorium on any attempt to extract some meaning from the event. For, if meaning were be attributed to it, it could only be the revealing of a bloodthirsty God who works out the greatest injustice in order to satisfy divine legal precepts. Rita Nakashima Brock even speaks provocatively about a cosmic divine "child abuse" as the one possible and appalling meaning to be deduced from the cross.[10] Philosophically this position was forcefully sustained by Max Horkheimer when he defended the nonredeemability of all past suffering, the impossibility to do justice for past victims, and, therefore, the meaninglessness of their victimization: "Past injustice has occurred and is closed. Those who were slain in it were truly slain."[11]

Nietzsche and the Critique of Dolorism

The second critique of the cross since the Enlightenment is raised by Friedrich Nietzsche (though announced earlier by young Hegelians like Feuerbach and Bruno Bauer). The cross is a sign of defeat sublimated in a slave morality that leads to defeatism, to the glorification of weakness perpetuating the mentality of an anemic will. If the first critique reacted against the image of God obtained from an objective theory of atonement (as in Anselm, for example), the Nietzschean line of argumentation denounces the cross for its mystification of suffering and for its perpetuation of a lack of will to make the world different: "Christianity is called the religion of compassion. Compassion or pity stands in opposition

[8] Choan Seng Song, "Christian Mission toward Abolition of the Cross," in *The Scandal of a Crucified World: Perspectives on the Cross and Suffering*, ed. Yacob Tesfai (Maryknoll, N.Y.: Orbis Books, 1994), 14.

[9] Joanne Carlson Brown and Rebecca Parker, "For God So Loved the World?" in Joanne Carlson Brown and Carole R. Bohn, eds., *Christianity, Patriarchy, and Abuse: A Feminist Critique* (Cleveland: Pilgrim Press, 1989), 27.

[10] Rita Nakashima Brock, "And a Little Child Will Lead Us," in ibid., 52.

[11] Cited by Helmut Peukert, *Science, Action, and Fundamental Theology: Toward a Theology of Communicative Action* (Cambridge: MIT Press, 1984), 206f.

to resolute fervor, which lifts up the energy of liveliness; it is depressive. One loses energy when one is compassionate."[12] It attests to the failure of gathered will and drains away self-confidence. "Christianity is the hatred turned against the spirit, against pride, courage, freedom, against the libertinage of the spirit; Christianity is the hatred of the senses, of the sensual pleasures, of happiness above all."[13]

The Nietzschean line of argumentation criticizes precisely the relationship between the cross and Jesus' teachings that Lessing and his followers found as the redeeming feature of Christianity. For Nietzsche the cross is itself the demonstration of the effects the slave mentality that Jesus' teachings have had, producing an anemic will, unable and unwilling to assert itself except in a permanent and corrosive resentment. Unlike the criticism of the tragic death, Nietzsche sees the cross as being definitely linked to Jesus' life, offering a key to read his teaching, and this key is defeatism and dolorism.

> This "happy preacher" died as he lived, as he taught—not "to redeem humankind," but to show what is left in life. This practice is what he left as his heritage: his attitude before the judges; before his snatchers; before his accusers and all types of slander and scorn—his attitude in the cross. He did not resist, he did not defend his rights, he did not take a single step to prevent his fate, even more, he demanded it....And he begged, he suffered, he loved with those, in those who did him evil. Not to defend himself, not to be enraged, not to take up responsibility....Not even to resist evil—but love it....The Gospel died in the cross....The fate of the Gospel decided itself for death, it hangs in the "cross."[14]

If a version of the tragic-death argument can be found in Peter's rebuttal to Jesus announcement of his passion, the defeatist argument can be seen somehow prefigured in what we know about the community in Corinth from Paul's first letter to them. They were spiritualists of Gnostic persuasion for which the body was a sort of an afterthought of the spirit.

---

[12] Friedrich Nietzsche, *Werke in zwei Bänden* (Leipzig: Alfred Kröner, 1930), 2:215.

[13] Ibid., 2:223.

[14] Ibid., 2:229–30.

To them Paul insisted that the body is a temple from and for God (1 Cor. 6:19); the physical comes first, then the spiritual (15:19). They celebrated the *power* of the *message* of the resurrection without the physical cross. To them Paul said that he did not want to know anything but Christ and him crucified (2:2). Nietzsche certainly did not share with them the Gnostic disregard for the body, but he celebrated with them the freedom of the spirit, that "libertinage of the spirit" (Nietzsche) by which "all things are lawful" (6:12).

Some theologians have affirmed a similar criticism and have found in the resurrection accounts the necessary correction to that in the cross itself which cannot be redeemed. While "Christianity is an abusive theology that glorifies suffering,"[15] the resurrection is the answer to Nietzsche, showing that Christianity, while deserving the philosopher's reproach, need not succumb to it. One must emphasize in the Christian story that

> death is overcome when human beings choose life, refusing the threat of death. Jesus climbed out of the grave…when he refused to abandon his commitment to the truth even though his enemies *threatened* him with death. On Good Friday, the Resurrected One was crucified.[16]

Instead of following the Enlightenment's escape to the moral life and teachings of the earthly Jesus, this line of argument moves from the cross to the resurrection, affirming the vigor of a defiant life in which the resurrection logically precedes the crucifixion and overshadows it. The fixation on the cross demonstrates the strength to fight for life and attests only to a defeat that should never be the central message, much less the last word. The cross should never have the primacy of shaping Christian discourse. In the words of Rev. Johnny Youngblood:

> An over-concentration on the cross—the suffering of Jesus Christ, has been a part of the spiritual abuse of racistic religion as perpetrated against people of color. This over-concentration has led to a sense of

---

[15] Brown and Parker, "For God So Loved the World?" 26.
[16] Ibid., 28.

earned powerlessness as well as a learned powerlessness, and all of that can be erased and healed…in the light of the resurrection.[17]

The Responses

In modern times the rediscovery of the theology of the cross is a reaction against precisely these two criticisms. As David Tracy notes, the theology of the cross, while essential, is a minority tradition in Christian theology.[18] One might say that it is evoked in times of theological and ecclesial crises, and it fades in times of theological and ecclesiastical "stability" or "normalcy." Both of the criticisms we have discussed represent such a crisis in ecclesio-theological stability, disturbing incisions in the stable body politic of the church and the theological academy.

As compelling as the critical arguments are, they have been met with no less potent apologies for the centrality of the cross in Christian theology and practice. Two discreet attempts to interpret the cross in contemporary theology are reactions corresponding to the two critiques. These responses have as their forerunners the two so-called master narratives that attempted to reconstruct and advance modernity's possibilities and promises. They are philosophical, not theological in the strict sense of the term. Yet theologians turned to them to support their pleas for a theology of the cross.

Hegel and the Speculative Good Friday

As a response to the criticism leveled by the Enlightenment's tragic-death argument we have what is called the trinitarian line of reasoning. Its source is G. W. F. Hegel's reconstruction of the philosophy of history as a record of the life of Spirit actualizing itself in the world in a process that entails negation and the negation of negation. In his lectures on philosophy of religion Hegel offers the basic template theologians have

---

[17] Johnny Youngblood, "Growing in the Power of the 'Resurrected' Christ," *Punctuations* (April 16, 1995), 5.

[18] Center for Theological Inquiry, David Tracy, *Form and Fragment* (22 March 2002); available online from www.ctinquiry.org/publications/reflections_volume_3/tracy.htm (accessed 6 July 2006).

used to reconstruct a theology with the cross at its center—the necessary culmination of Jesus' life and teaching and the indispensable transition to a bright new reality.

> *God has died, God is dead*: this is the most frightful of all thoughts, that everything eternal and true does not exist, that negation itself is found in God....However, the process does not halt at this point; rather, a reversal takes place....God rises again to life, and thus things are reversed.[19]

In response to the charge that with the cross the God of love is surrendered by a brutal act in which God is also implicated, he writes: "The monstrous unification of these absolute extremes is love itself.—[This is the] speculative way of perceiving things."[20]

This "speculative Good Friday," as he called it, affirms, as one of Hegel's contemporary poets phrased it, that "where danger lies grows also what saves."[21] Hegel's appeal to theology is undeniable, not because of his complex metaphysics but because his simple structure focuses on the evangelical narrative in which life is negated by death and affirmed in a life on a higher level: the glorified and resurrected Christ. This higher level is conveyed by Hegel's key technical notion of *Aufhebung*, often translated in English as "sublation," which entails both cancellation of the former stage and its simultaneous elevation to a higher level.

There is an internal logic of reversals within the divine economy or the life of Spirit in history that follows the Hippocratic maxim: "the opposite cures the opposite" (*contraria contrariis curantur*). The cross becomes a necessary dialectical movement.[22] For Hegel, this form of rendering

---

[19] Georg Wilhelm Friedrich Hegel, *Christian Religion: Lectures on the Philosophy of Religion*, ed. Peter C. Hodgson (Missoula: Scholars Press, 1979), 212.

[20] Ibid., 202.

[21] Friedrich Hölderlin, "Patmos" in *Gedichte/Hyperion* (Augsburg: Wilhelm Goldmann, 1978), 138.

[22] Karl Löwith comments about Hegel's famous proposition that *die Weltgeschichte ist das Weltgericht* (the history of the world is the world's judgment), and as he remarked: "Hegel believed himself loyal to the genius of Christianity by realizing the Kingdom of God on earth. And, since he transposed the Christian expectation of a final consummation into the historical process as such, he saw the world's history as consummating itself." Löwith, *Meaning in History* (Chicago: Phoenix, 1964), 57–58.

immanent the eschatological moment is totally reasonable. It is what he means by "the speculative way of perceiving things." For him "the *logical necessity*, …the reasonable…alone is the *speculative*."[23]

Hegel claims to be capable of overcoming the disjunction between love and wrath, salvation and condemnation, compassion and justice, by placing them within the economic Trinity as it unfolds itself immanently within history. In doing so, he is able to address the Enlightenment's criticism that the cross makes love and wrath mutually exclusive.

There is a price to be paid, however. Hegel does not address a related criticism that refers to the sociocultural impact of the cross. It was indeed scandalous and foolish, and attempts to reason it out by saying that the one hanging on the cross was really not God or really not human were readily available. In this reasoning the scandal and the folly were kept even if later sublimated. In Hegel, scandal and folly become speculative, that is, entirely reasonable; suffering is rendered downright logical. Here what we called the ironic and destabilizing gesture of the cross is inserted into a new and stable system. It creates what Oswald Bayer called, not without ironic overtones, a *theologia crucis naturalis*, a natural theology of the cross.[24] Suffering is an inherent part of the structure of a natural theology of the cross; the immediate meaning to all suffering, as if it were grafted to unyielding, even callous logical law. In this theology of the cross, the scandal is built into the speculative movement of the trinitarian economy itself.

Nevertheless, the genius of Hegel was to offer theologians a way of speaking about the cross that avoids its sublimation and connects the cross of Jesus with the crosses of the world. Hegel's system flirts with Gnosticism with its quasi-denial of real suffering, insofar as the cross is for him a logical and necessary moment in the self-actualization of the Spirit. In spite of this, and shunning Hegel's metaphysical speculation (at least intending to), theologians have taken from the philosopher a basic impulse. The Lutheran Hegel provided a way of relating the theology of the cross to Luther's third mode of Christ's physical ("according to his

---

[23] Georg Wilhelm Friedrich Hegel, *Werke* (Frankfurt a/M: Suhrkamp, 1979), 3:55.

[24] Oswald Bayer, *Gott als Autor: Zu einer poietologischen Theologie* (Tübingen: Mohr-Siebeck, 1999), 258–59.

humanity") presence, the mode by which Christ, without the separation of the two natures, is "present in all created things....You must place this existence of Christ...far, far beyond things created, as far as God transcends them; and, on the other hand, place it as deep in and as near to all created things as God is in them."[25] If this is the case, the crucified Christ is present, as crucified, in the crosses of this world, nearer to the pain as anyone can be.

Marx and the Response of Praxis

As a response to dolorism or the Nietzsche-inspired criticism of the cross as defeatism, we have what could be called the praxiological argument. This is the other great movement in the recovery of the theology of the cross. It sets out from the criticism the young Karl Marx precisely raised against Hegel. He calls for a critical philosophy that shuns Hegel's sublation (*Aufhebung*) of the religious dogmas, including doctrines about cross and atonement, into speculative truth. For Marx the task requires something else. In his words: "Criticism has plucked the imaginary flowers from the chain not so that man will wear the chain without any fantasy or consolation, but so that he will shake off the chain and cull the living flower."[26] For Marx, Hegel's system plucked the chimerical flowers of religious flights of the imagination from the chains of strictly logical historical events and pronounced the knowledge of this staunch logic to be real freedom without changing anything because it was a logical necessity. Marx, for whom Prometheus was the most important saint in the philosophical calendar, did not think so. Like Prometheus, who stole fire from the monopoly of the gods to give to humans, Marx stormed the heavens of the Hegelian absolute system and pronounced, with clear apocalyptic overtones, the whole of human history, enclosed

---

[25] Martin Luther, "Confession Concerning Christ's Supper (1528)," *Luther's Works* vol. 37 *Word and Sacament III*, ed. and trans. Robert H. Fischer (Philadelphia: Fortress Press, 1961), 223.

[26] Karl Marx and Friedrich Engels, *Basic Writings on Politics and Philosophy*, ed. Lewis Feuer (New York: Anchor, 1959), 263 (from "Toward the Critique of Hegel's Philosophy of Right").

by Hegel in his system, a prehistory. History was just beginning. This beginning happens when people realize that the world is not to be merely interpreted but transformed.

Marx, in fact, anticipates a response to Nietzsche. His response would have been nonacceptance of suffering, which Hegel rationalized and Nietzsche only denounced, whether in church doctrine or in philosophical systems. For Marx there was a Promethean alternative: insurrection! History was not closed. What can be imagined might be done.

It took more than a century for theologians to seize the idea. The resurrection of Jesus was an insurrection. It defied the obdurate laws of the world to the point where even the last invincible enemy—death—is overcome. And if the resurrection was an insurrection, then insurrections are, theologically rendered, resurrections. Here theology responds also to Marx by radicalizing his claim. History is not only open to the future but also to the past. It is necessary to reveal the memory of the chains, of the crosses of this world, to remind the powers that "suffering has no meaning, but might have a future."[27] In the words of Jewish German and Marxian thinker Walter Benjamin, influential among many theologians even when regarding himself a historical materialist: "The work of the past is not closed for the historical materialist. He cannot see the work of an epoch, or any part of it, as reified, as literally placed on one's lap."[28] And for Benjamin this openness was that which allowed justice even for the victims of the past.

With this appropriation and reinterpretation of Marx there is place for a theology of the cross, a restricted but important one. Cross and suffering that lies in the past can be recalled, and because it can be recalled it has a future, for we are reminded of this by the message of the resurrection. The resurrection of Jesus is the key by which past victims, through memory, are given a future that remains open. The past is not closed and it can be undone insofar as it can be remembered. When it is remembered,

---

[27] Johann Baptist Metz, *Faith in History and Society* (New York: Seabury, 1980), 109.
[28] Walter Benjamin, *Ausgewählte Schriften II* (Frankfurt: Suhrkamp, 1955), 311.

the powers that produce victimization and count on forgetfulness are doomed—then and now. The words of the Apostle Paul eloquently express this conviction: "None of the rulers of this age understood this; for if they had, they would not have crucified the Lord of glory" (1 Cor. 2:8). This is a motif often turned to by theologians who do not disparage the use of the cross but are very cautious about its abuses.[29]

Epistemic Queries

Two critiques and two responses are used here as ideal types. Ideals types are analogous to caricatures, they are not portrayals of every nuance and detail. They are heuristic devices that magnify distinctive features and intentionally obliterate less relevant characteristics of what is depicted, features that have a *Wirkungsgeschichte*, an effective impact on the subsequent history of ideas and can be easily and distinctively recognized in them. This means there is a gist in Lessing and the Enlightenment that brings the tragic death argument to the forefront, a tenor that provokes Nietzsche's evocation of the motif of dolorism. Neither of these exhaust their positions or explain other aspects of their works. *Mutatis mutandis*, the same must be said of Hegel and Marx to characterize the sources of ensuing implicit apologies an array of theologians made explicit.

In this typological pairing of critiques and responses, however, it is relevant that the responses have been and are trapped within the parameters of the questions that prompted them. For the Enlightenment, the problem of the cross was a *moral* one: What can we learn from the cross that will teach us how to live? The implied assumption went from the denial of any moral lesson to an affirmation of Jesus' teachings, in the face of which the cross was little more than a tragic, inconsequential accident. The Hegelian-inspired response was to cast it in a dialectical frame as the necessary negation that brings about sublation (*Aufhebung*).

---

[29] Above all we should mention the work of Johann Baptist Metz (particularly *Faith in History and Society*). Others that find themselves in his company are Dorothee Sölle, Jon Sobrino (in his more recent works as *Jesus the Liberator, Christ the Liberator,* and *The Principle of Mercy*), Douglas John Hall, Mary Solberg, and Sally Purvis.

For Nietzsche, on the other hand, the problem was an *ontological* one: Who am I and what can I become in face of the cross? The assumption ranged from a resented self, anemic in its will and impotent to resist evil by sublimating and glorifying the cross, to affirmation of the imaginative and self-asserting power of the resurrection before the cross. The Marxian-inspired responses took the cross to be a description of the conditions of the oppressed people of the world that had to be named in order for a practice of liberation to follow. What has not been discussed in this entire context is a third question, exactly the one that guided Paul and Luther: What can I know of God in face of the cross or according to the cross (*kata stauron*)? This is the epistemological question that we will examine next.

Knowledge and Suffering

Epistemological Implications of the Cross

The person who looks on the visible rearward parts of God as seen in suffering and the cross does deserve to be called a theologian.

Martin Luther

We bring different questions to the cross, just as the cross addresses questions to us. The maze in which these questions inscribe themselves makes us feel like Theseus in the Greek myth, lost in the labyrinth without Ariadne's thread to find our way out. But the issues are too important for us to despair; we must tackle them with seriousness. Our effort here offers one way to organize the questions raised by the cross. The nature of our questions will shape the answers that ensue. These questions take three forms, employing three basic keys to read the meaning of the cross.

The Apoteletic Key

The first of these questions comes from an ontological perspective that asks what the cross is in and of itself. The answers take varied shapes, always understanding that it is an event that had to happen in fulfillment of the divine economy. It can be defined as an act of atonement, a sacrifice, an offering of satisfaction, a battle lost to the devil for the sake of triumphing in the war against evil,[1] and so forth. These questions call for the formulation of different motifs and models of objective theories of atonement. Looking at the cross of Jesus in terms of what it accomplishes does not require affection or our subjective disposition toward it.

We can say these questions have an *apoteletic* key (the Greek *apoteleo*, means "to accomplish," "to bring to an end," or "to perform"). Apoteletic questions are those that ask what the cross accomplishes, how its economy works, what the cross brings about, and what objective difference it makes for the world that Jesus died as he did. The answers to these questions are largely determined by the questions themselves. They also presuppose that this knowledge is somehow available in an objective manner. To put it theologically, the revelation through which God imparts this knowledge is contained within the domain of what Scriptures and tradition have kept and made available to us. Whether or not we accept it does not change what it is.

Criticisms that focus on the glorification of the cross, and the problem of sliding into the assumption that all suffering is redeeming, are really criticisms of the answers offered within this apoteletic key. These criticisms, however, do not challenge the presupposition that leads to the apoteletic answers: the essential and sacramental connectedness between the cross of Calvary and human suffering that makes all suffering identical with Jesus' suffering.

As Nietzsche has shown, glorification of the cross surrenders our will to change our own condition. In the words of the *saeta*, which Antonio Machado criticized, we keep asking for a "ladder to get up the cross and pull off the nails of Jesus the Nazarene." But it is this perennially suffering Christ, "always with blood in his hands, always waiting to be released," which elicits a devotion of suffering that will last as long as Jesus is not released. He never is; this is the condition that sustains the devotion.

An example of this approach, which tries to correct the dolorism and defeatism decried in the apoteletic key, is Danish theologian Regin Prenter's interpretation of Luther's theology of the cross. He starts

---

[1] This is the theory of atonement that Gustaf Aulén attributed to Irenaeus, among other early Christian fathers, in *Christus Victor* (New York: Macmillan, 1969).

from the basic thesis that for Luther the cross of Christ is essentially "identical...with the cross we are called upon to bear."[2] The cross has no relevance in Christian theology except in connection with our own suffering, a suffering that is universal, presumably due to the human fall. The argument is circular. The cross acquires meaning only in the context of the sacramental practice of baptism (dying to sin in Christ) and the eucharist (being raised to and participating in the glorious body of Christ). For Prenter the cross is universally true and necessary for salvation if we recognize ourselves to be under God's judgment in the midst of the world's suffering, of which we are victims and agents alike. The cross of Christ is identical with ours; by the latter God works redemption through the former. By our crosses we are led to the cross of Christ in daily baptism. The cross of Christ establishes that in that cross sin, which is our cross, has been defeated. By anticipation, proleptically, our suffering has already been conquered. Suffering acquires meaning because its power is cancelled in the justifying word of God that is announced in baptism, to which we daily return. Prenter attempts to correct the Hegelian "natural theology of the cross" by connecting the necessary trinitarian economy with an existential or circumstantial component that links the dialectics of the cross with the experience of it in daily life.

Prenter remains subject to Oswald Bayer's criticism of the "natural theology of the cross," however, when he reduces the meaning of suffering to sin, that is, to the universal human condition. Once the whole human condition of suffering is leveled, with no distinction in the suffering, there is no difference as to who imposes suffering; all are equally victims and victimizers; everything comes down to a sacramental act of dying in sin with Christ for a new life. The cross, Prenter writes,

---

[2] Regin Prenter, *Luther's Theology of the Cross* (Philadelphia: Fortress Press, 1971), 3. In fact, Luther's interchangeable use of cross, suffering, and death suggests that their use in reference to Christ can also be figuratively transferred to human suffering. But more than once Luther admonishes not to mix the cross of Christ with ours. See, e.g., *WA* 7, 102, 103. Cf. Dorothee Sölle, *Leiden* (Stuttgart: Kreuz-Verlag, 1973), 161.

comes to us through the trials and temptations of our lives, and precisely because it comes over us and is not chosen by us, the cross we are called upon to bear is in a mysterious way identical with the cross of Christ. God lays his cross upon us for our salvation; the sinner is crucified that the new justified man may arise.[3]

For Prenter the cross of Christ has in itself no soteriological significance except for its essential identity with our own crosses. This reduction fails to account for the senseless suffering of innocent victims who cannot relate their own suffering to the death of sin in the cross of Jesus. The problem of Job, the lament of the innocent victim, is not addressed by Prenter. His solution, while avoiding a pure objective dialectic of suffering and redemption (and therefore of making suffering in itself atoning) tends to write off the meaninglessness of suffering by sacramentalizing it. Any suffering and all suffering is leveled in order to find a universal common denominator that allows us all to share equally in Christ's own passion. Christ's cross becomes the first among equals (*primus inter paribus*) for defining suffering.

The Moral Key

The second form these questions take comes from the moral approach. Here the questions are more like, what does the cross move me to do? In an apoteletic key the cross is seen primarily in a sacramental way; in the moral key it has an exemplary character; instructing one on how to live and act. The answers to the apoteletic questions presuppose the essential connectedness between the cross of Calvary and human suffering in general. The moral questions move swiftly to an analogical connection between the historical cross of Jesus and human suffering; the cross becomes a metaphor for human suffering in general. Criticisms focusing on the mystification of suffering and acceptance of implied redemptive

---

[3] Prenter, *Luther's Theology of the Cross*, 13.

meaning in suffering itself presume this moral key for reading the cross. Joanne Carlson Brown and Rebecca Parker's criticism of the "moral influence" theory of atonement is an example:

> The moral influence theory is founded on the belief that an innocent, suffering victim and only an innocent, suffering victim for whose suffering we are in some way responsible has the power to confront us with our guilt and move us to a new decision. This belief has subtle and terrifying connections as to how victims of violence can be viewed.[4]

Jon Sobrino, a Jesuit theologian from El Salvador, tries to avoid the pitfalls of the "moral influence" theory while working within its parameters. He confesses his preference for the "Lutheran" emphasis on the theology of the cross in rejecting theodicy and atonement theories, in spite of criticism he has received for this stance.[5] Like Prenter, he tries to combine the particularity of the cross of Jesus with its universal salvific meaning. He does not identify the cross of Christ with our own crosses, however, and so avoids diminishing suffering to sin and reducing redemption to sacramental participation. Sobrino speaks of an "analogous"[6] relation between the crucified people and the Jesus of the cross. He accomplishes the analogy by describing the poor and oppressed, the "crucified people," as passive martyrs of the faith, who "are the ones who most abundantly and cruelly 'fill up in their flesh what is lacking in Christ's passion.' They are the Suffering Servant and they are the Crucified Christ today."[7]

Sobrino thus attributes meaning to suffering in this way: as God has participated in the suffering of the Son, so God is also by analogy a cosufferer with the crucified people. Avoiding a sacramental resolution that identifies our suffering with Christ's, a "resurrectionism" (Douglas John

---

[4] Joanne Carlson Brown and Rebecca Parker, "For God So Loved the World?" in Joanne Carlson Brown and Carole R. Bohn, eds., *Christianity, Patriarchy, and Abuse* (Cleveland: Pilgrim Press, 1989), 12.

[5] Jon Sobrino, *Jesus the Liberator* (Maryknoll, N.Y.: Orbis Books, 1993), 235.

[6] Ibid., 269–71.

[7] Ibid., 271.

Hall) that cancels the scandal, his solution recognizes the particularity of suffering. Sobrino tends to make suffering in itself atoning, however, while the experience of forsakenness in the cross seems to be only apparent or at most temporary. In this context he can say that "the only suffering that has meaning is the suffering for the sake of struggling against suffering."[8] Hence, if this suffering for the sake of fighting suffering has meaning, it must be also redeeming, in analogy to the suffering of Christ. But this affirmation entangles Sobrino in contradiction for he has to admit that those who are the principles in his analogy (*analogatum princeps*) are passive victims.[9] But how can a *passive* victim be fighting *against* suffering? Sobrino cannot avoid the problem of the moral influence that ultimately makes suffering as such redeeming, even if by its exemplary character.

These two, the sacramental and the exemplary approaches, under the apoteletic and the moral key respectively, are of decisive importance. Since Augustine the tradition has oscillated between these two, what the cross accomplishes by itself and what it moves us to do, often trying to combine them. These are the two "faces" of Christ's cross that Luther distinguishes carefully while affirming both under the categories of *sacramentum* and *exemplum*.[10]

Toward an Epistemic Key

While these attempts at realizing meaning in discussing the relationship between cross and suffering are important, we need to understand just what they are. They are discourses about cross and suffering, very much like the one we are engaged in with this very text. They are not the reality as such (Sobrino would be the first to recognize this). As simple as this might seem, it is a very complex problem, complex because that which

---

[8] Ibid., 241 (he attributes this idea to Dorothee Sölle; cf. Sölle, *Leiden*, 217).

[9] Ibid., 270.

[10] See Hubertus Blaumeiser, *Martin Luthers Kreuzestheologie: Schlüssel zu seiner Deutung von Mensch und Wirklichkeit. Eine Untersuchung anhand der Operationes in Psalmos (1519–1521)* (Paderborn: Bonifatius, 1995), 368–88.

precedes discourse can only be manifest in discourse itself. Hence, what the discourse unveils it simultaneously conceals. This is what is meant when it is said that the limit of our language is the limit of our world (Heidegger[11]). This limit is a veil which conceals that which only breaks through when the veil is ripped, properly called *re-velation*. But this is not our doing, it proceeds from above, as symbolized by the curtain of the Temple veiling the Holy of Holies, which is torn from top to bottom (Mark 15:38). This limit is *ours*.

Nevertheless, through discourse we try to frame a world for others to accept. A discourse is a linguistic strategy for imposing a world that *makes* sense;[12] this is its function. The discourses about cross and suffering (Luther called them *praedicare passionem*) are attempts at "making sense," of creating a world we can rely upon and administer. This effort is neither good nor evil in itself; it is simply our condition, the condition we are in before we even speak about it in discerning good and evil. What is important is the realization that "our" world, framed by the discourses we inhabit, is *ours* and not necessarily the *other*'s. The other might very well inhabit another discourse, another "world."

A simile can illustrate the difference between sheer, prelinguistic experience and its linguistic rendition in discourse. Consider, for example, the distinction between the experience that one has in gazing at a landscape and then taking a picture of it and sharing it with people who have not been on the site where the picture was taken. A good photographer would tell us that the clue to the meaning of a photo lies not only in what is captured in the picture, but in the angle, light, focus, and, most important, the frame in which it will be placed. The image one captures receives its meaning from the way one poses its limitations, sets a frame to it. So, when one sees a photograph taken by someone else, the range of meanings

---

[11] Martin Heidegger, *Existence and Being* (Chicago: Gateway, 1962), 276. See also Vítor Westhelle, "Communication and the Transgression of Language in Martin Luther," *Lutheran Quarterly* XVII, no. 1 (Spring 2003): 25.

[12] "To make something that has an enduring impact on the senses" is the technical meaning of the Greek word *poiesis* (the etymological origin of the word *poetry*).

she can take from it is conditioned—both limited and magnified—by the choices made earlier by the one who originally experienced the landscape and made choices about how to convey its meaning by framing it in a certain way, picturing it through certain lenses.

Meaningful knowledge is as much about perception as it is about exclusion. It is as much about presence as it is about absence (exclusion of what is deemed irrelevant or diversionary). The original choice of the frame does not block the way to finding alternative meanings, but it limits and conditions them. The point is that a certain portrayal of any event excludes other knowledges—and this very act of presenting and or concealing has its own set of questions, the epistemological questions. These questions lead us; they condition our interpretation. Every discourse functions like a picture of a reality experienced. Before we ask for the meaning of a discourse, like the ways of defining the relation between cross and suffering, we need to identify this act of presenting and or concealing. We need to observe what is being done in the cutting (framing?) of the scene and what it means. Because we inhabit one or many pictures we are blind to their margins; they are the limits of our world, veiling otherness. We only encounter these limits when we transgress them.

This example is obviously an oversimplification but it helps us think about a literary text like the Bible, with its manifold and moving frames. The implied question in any search for meaning is found in the limits in a body of knowledge we discursively receive. It is not only the question of the portrayal of the cross (literary or artistic); it is the very question the cross itself evokes. The cross itself, the event of the cross, presents the problem of the frame, the problem of representation. Reading the Heidelberg Disputation in its entirety, not only the famous theses about the theologian of the cross, we must be struck by the amazing way Luther struggles to push us to the discursive frames of the established epistemes (philosophy and reason) of economy (works and labor), politics (justice and equity), and the church (sin and grace). He works to move us beyond and behind the canvas of the artist to see what might have been (and in his case certainly had been) excluded from the frame, or put in a dim light.

I have called this a transgressive knowledge[13]—a theologian of the cross should constantly transgress the limits of accepted epistemes, either to corroborate the decision to convey that frame of meanings or to criticize it. Other theologians have called it "epistemological break,"[14] the moment when a conventional meaning breaks apart to open new possibilities.

The theology of the cross as an epistemological gesture places the question of the relationship between cross and suffering on another key. It is not necessary to disavow the sacramental meaning (Prenter) nor the exemplary character it displays (Sobrino). It asks another set of questions: Why did Jesus die? Why do people suffer? and, What is the relationship between these two questions? A suggestive way toward an answer is that there is a concealed truth in suffering that risks disclosing the nature of our societal and human relations—discloses it in ways we might not otherwise endure.

An example of natural evil illustrates the point. Pain that I feel in my body is a signifier, a cipher to a physical disorder. The pain itself does not entail a meaning, except for allowing me to name my condition. This naming allows one to treat the cause. For the one suffering illness, however, this naming can be risky because it evokes powers beyond one's control, power to destroy a person as strong as the cause of the pain itself, as any person with AIDS knows. Like leprosy in biblical times, AIDS has a physiological and also a societal etiology; both conditions can break down interpersonal relations as surely as the disease corrodes the body.

Social and interpersonal suffering functions in a similar way. It is a symptom of a power that destroys and kills—destroys relations and kills the body. This power is what Paul calls the law; on one hand it manifests

---

[13] Vítor Westhelle, "Scientific Sight and Embodied Knowledges," *Modern Theology* 11, no. 3 (July 1995): 341–61.

[14] See Mary Solberg, *Compelling Knowledge: A Feminist Proposal for an Epistemology of the Cross* (Albany: State University of New York Press, 1997), 117–18. For a comprehensive study of theology as "epistemic rupture," see Clodovis Boff, *Teologia e Prática: Teologia do Político e suas Mediações* (Petrópolis: Vozes, 1978). The expression "epistemological break" or "epistemological mutation" comes from French philosopher Louis Althusser; see Althusser and Étienne Balibar, *Reading Capital* (London: NLB, 1975), 75, 109, 153, et passim. The basis for the concept is presented in Althusser, *For Marx* (New York: Vintage, 1970), 87–128.

our condition and on the other it threatens us with death. Paul's concept of the law that reveals our condition and hastens our destruction works in a similar way as epistemic frames in which we operate and that we take for granted. Jesus died on the cross because he named the law that kills and practiced the healing that restores. He did it by stepping precisely into the margin of the law, in one sense by radicalizing and stretching its meaning to the limits—as in the Sermon on the Mount—and in another sense by transgressing it—as in miracles or in the gracious forgiveness of sins.

Parrhesia

Let us examine this a little further. From the intertestamental period into the time of Jesus an apocalyptic theology developed that lies as background to the Gospel narrative. In the apocalyptic imagery marked by a conflict-ridden power structure was the idea that together with the advent of the Messiah would come an anti-Messiah, designated the blasphemer, the great gainsayer. Jesus' conflicts with the religious groups of his day are constantly set into this dispute: Is Jesus the Messiah or the blasphemer? The line dividing the two seems very thin, for the truth when boldly spoken might sound like apostasy. What brought Jesus to the cross was this accusation of blasphemy against God and the emperor, his boldness in saying plainly "what the thing is," as Luther said in thesis 21 of the Heidelberg Disputation: "A theologian of the cross calls the thing what it actually is." But what does it mean to call something what it actually is? What does it mean to say the truth? How can one afford it? When should one engage in it?

The messianic secret of the Gospel of Mark might help us to answer these questions. In Mark the identity of Jesus is intentionally concealed from the public until chapter 11, when Jesus enters Jerusalem, the final stage of his passion. Then the whole question about his legitimacy and his authority reaches a climax that unleashes the powers that would bring him to the cross. Jesus was executed just after he dared to tell the truth openly, no longer concealing it as a secret, because what he said was recognized as having authenticity; he said what he meant and he meant what he said. The concealment of the truth about himself allowed Jesus to elaborate his teachings and carry out his work in relative safety. The public disclosure of Jesus' identity at last precipitated his end. With the messianic secret, Mark suggests that for the sake of effectiveness there is a tactical need for reckoning the right time to exercise truth telling. It was only upon entering Jerusalem, the seat of power, that Jesus publicly proclaimed his messianic identity. The implication is that if it were done earlier the efficacy would be compromised. But how do we recognize when the time is ripe for truth to be exercised? Further, how do we recognize the type of truth speaking that can lead one to risk even one's own life? How is the Messiah to be distinguished from the blasphemer? Is there a rule that regulates this kind of speech?

In two of his last lectures at the Collège de France, the late French philosopher and social critic Michel Foucault engaged in an analysis of truth speaking going back to the ancient Greek concept of *parrhesia*, to speak the truth boldly, or plainly saying it all, without reserve.[15] His whole argument from these lectures cannot be fully rehearsed here, but it is interesting to lift up Foucault's analysis of the necessary connection between truth speaking and freedom. It is established by being part of a *demos*, a people in and through which one knows one's own belonging. The example he uses to conclude his study is illustrative; he comments on Euripides' play *Ion*. The title character in the play is in Athens looking for the mother he does not know. He hopes she would be an Athenian, otherwise, he says, he will not have the right to speak freely, boldly, and will be confined to the rules and laws of the city of men.

Ion says: "Even if the law itself would make a citizen of a stranger who enters a city, the possibility of speaking remains limited to the one of a slave; he would not have the right to say all freely."[16] Foucault is probably relying on the psychoanalytical distinction between the law of the father

---

[15] Michel Foucault, *Das Wahrsprechen des Anderen: Zwei Vorlesungen von 1983/84*, ed. Ulrike Reuter, Lothar Wolfstetter, Hermann Kocyba, and Bernd Heiter, trans. Ulrike Reuter with Lothar Wolfstetter (Frankfurt: Materialis, 1988), 15–42. See also his lectures at the University of California at Berkeley in the fall term of 1983, later published as *Fearless Speech*, ed. Joseph Pearson, (Los Angeles: Semiotext(e), 2001).

[16] Foucault, *Das Wahrsprechen*, 41.

and the language, the tongue, of the mother. This theme of Lacanian psychoanalysis links us to the discussion about the law that we had earlier. What matters is not the constitution of the law itself, its inner structure or its theme. The search for the mother "constitutes one's personality that gives the right to speak and binds one to the membership of a *demos*."[17] This and not the law is what grants one a language that can be authentically uttered without reserve, even by transgressing the law for the sake of authenticity.

Foucault distinguishes *parrhesia* accordingly from other regulated discursive genres (represented by the discourses employed by the "sage," the "prophet," and the "technician") and their discursive strategies (demonstration, rhetoric, pedagogy, and heuristics),[18] all of which have their own laws in which they are legitimized. This is what allows them to be analyzed from the perspective of the internal structure of the discourse, from its finality, the effect it produces and the intention of the enunciator. Like the law, both in the juridical or political and in the theological sense, all these strategies are inscribed in an economy of investiture in the expectation of a return, of a pay-off. But *parrhesia* is different; it does not invest in anything but itself. It does not imply a strategic calculation, it simply says a thing for what it is. "*Parrhesia* does not bring about any codified effect. It opens up an undefined risk."[19]

What one buys is not some other result but *parrhesia* itself. In it, a total expenditure implies a critical risk, the risk of saying things as they are, as Luther put it and as he practiced it with courage at Worms when he said: "Here I stand and can do no otherwise." Brazilian Bishop Dom Helder Câmara expressed this well when he said: "When I feed the hungry they call me a saint; when I ask why they are hungry, they call me a communist." This is again the "Why?" question, the one the *parrhesiast* addresses.

Only from the perspective of risk and danger, Foucault tells us, can *parrhesia* be read. "The parrhesiasts are those who undertake the truth

---

[17] Ibid., 42.

[18] Michel Foucault, *Archeology of Knowledge* (New York: Pantheon, 1972).

[19] Foucault, *Das Wahrsprechen*, 32.

speaking and for that they will have to pay a price that has not been determined in advance, but can imply even their death."[20] The telling of a story is not all that is implied here, but also the circumstances in which it happens, the powers it conjures, the forces it releases.

Indian theologian M. M. Thomas reflected on the cross as *parrhesia* long before Foucault made the term available to describe the risky action of speaking the truth. Thomas used Mahatma Gandhi's principle of *satyagraha*. *Satyagraha* is a Sanskrit word (from *satya* = truth/love derived from *Sat* meaning being, and *agraha* = firmness/force), which roughly translated means truth-force, force that comes from adhering to truth. For Gandhi it "literally translated as insistence on truth."[21] Truth for Gandhi was soul or spirit and hence *satyagraha* came to be known as soul-force: a force that is to violence, tyranny and all injustice, what light is to darkness. The principle of *satyagraha* came into being in distinction to the notion of passive resistance. For Gandhi, the term *passive resistance* was too narrowly construed, characterized by hatred, and could manifest itself into violence whereas *satyagraha* operated on the principle of "vindication of truth not by infliction of suffering on the opponent but on one's self."[22] *Satyagraha* implies a search for truth and a determination to reach the truth. It demands truth, refusal to inflict injury upon others, and willingness for self-sacrifice. For Thomas *satyagraha* was an illustration of the symbol of the cross, where God meets evil with a "transcendent *satyagraha*."

For the theologian, the fearlessness that comes out of the power of truth might appear as a defeat, but a defeat undertaken for the sake of overcoming evil itself. "The *satyagrahi's* greatest assurance is that the cause for which he stands will win ultimately, though he may fail for the moment."[23] *Satyagraha*, in the sense Thomas uses it, adds to the notion of *parrhesia* not only the risk that it entails but also the prospect of a defeat in the trust that no act of love will ultimately fail.[24]

[20] Ibid., 31.

[21] M. K. Gandhi, *Non-Violent Resistance (Satyagraha)* (New York: Schocken, 1961), 78.

[22] Ibid., 6.

[23] M. M. Thomas, *Ideological Quest Within Christian Commitment 1939–1954*, (CISRS, Bangalore: The Christian Literature Society, Madras, 1983), 10.

[24] Ibid.

Truth speaking demands willingness to sacrifice and is framed in a context of risk—the risk of defeat, taken for the sake of the truth. This spirit-filled circumstance (the spirit of truth and wisdom of 1 Corinthians 2) implies an existential decision, however, a moment of "madness," as Kierkegaard called it. It has characteristics of madness and entails a scandal, as Paul recognized, exactly because it is an utterance that comes at a certain point where the "law" (the prevailing systems of the world) is stretched to its limit and finally transgressed. But much more than this it is a way of unmasking the powers and producing healing. New Testament scholar Gerd Theissen, commenting on 2 Corinthians 2:6-16, implies a "cognitive" restructuring of our perception of the world: "The cross was foolishness in the world as traditionally interpreted. In it the cross was cognitively dissonant."[25] Salvation comes through its opposite. "The striving for salvation can be realized only in a paradoxical manner, namely, through liberation from the compulsion of the prevailing system of convictions."[26] This is what Paul recognized when speaking about the word of the cross, and he concludes: "None of the rulers of this age understood this; for if they had, they would not have crucified the Lord of glory" (1 Cor. 2:8). The cross names the world for what it is, a naming "from below" (Theissen) that breaks into the systems of knowledge, convictions, and power.

The *logos tou staurou* is about this naming. And it was not just a neutral naming, an ideological criticism of the system, religious or political. It was that too, but the point that brought dispute about Jesus' credentials and the accusations of blasphemy were most often connected with Jesus' healing practice and exorcisms, his concern for the sick and outcast. In short, the words, the naming that brought Jesus to the cross, were words addressing human suffering. So the relationship between Jesus' suffering and passion and the suffering people in the world today is neither one of identity like in Prenter, nor an analogical relationship like in Sobrino. Sharply put, Jesus died because he addressed his words to the suffering of the people. Here the distinction that the late poet Audre Lorde draws

---

[25] Gerd Theissen, *Psychological Aspects of Pauline Theology* (Philadelphia: Fortress Press, 1987), 387.
[26] Ibid., 392.

between suffering and pain is instructive. Even if the concepts she uses to make the distinction might not be the most helpful ones the distinction is pertinent:

> There is a distinction I am beginning to make in my living between *pain* and *suffering*. Pain is an event, an experience that must be recognized, named, and then used in some way in order for the experience to change, to be transformed into something else, strength or knowledge or action. Suffering, on the other hand, is the nightmare reliving of unscrutinized and unmetabolized pain. When I live through pain without recognizing it, self-consciously, I rob myself of the power that can come from *using* that pain, the power to fuel some movement beyond it.[27]

There is indeed one type of suffering that remains within a certain logic that turns it into a normal thing, inscribing it into certain legislation, a law that prevents it from being addressed, owned, and fought. There is another type of suffering (or a pain, according to Lorde) that results from addressing the root causes of precisely the first type of suffering. Suffering might be only passive and mute endurance; pain, for Lorde, is suffering that is named. This is the answer to the question addressed earlier to Sobrino about the difference between suffering in itself and suffering undergone to overcome it. The suffering that is not redeeming is the one that becomes a "law" that makes one endure it as the way things are. The suffering that fights suffering is the one that comes as a consequence of stretching the "law" to its limits and transgressing it, trespassing the boundaries of the ruling narrative itself, or what Theissen called "the cognitive dissonance that came into the world through Christ. This dissonance was triggered by the cross."[28]

Jesus suffered because he named the cause of suffering, the law that kills. And in this naming lies the power to overcome it. The power of

---

[27] Audre Lorde, *Sister Outsider: Essays and Speeches* (Freedom, Calif.: Crossing, 1984), 171–72.

[28] Theissen, *Psychological Aspects*, 386. See also Alexandra R. Brown, *The Cross and Human Transformation: Paul's Apocalyptic Word in 1 Corinthians* (Minneapolis: Fortress Press, 1993), 157–60. Theories of cognitive dissonance operate with a triadic logic that can be generally put in the following formula: "A" disapproves of "X" but approves of "B." The dissonance comes when "A" learns that "B" approves of "X." In the case of the experience with the cross of Jesus it takes the following syllogism:

the cross teaches us to recognize where this naming comes from and where we need to stand in order to exercise it, teaches us when the occasions in which this naming should happen are, when they are an effective *satyagraha*. To understand the problem with the apocalyptic distinction between the Messiah and the blasphemer is not difficult, for, in fact, the two are equally true depending on where one stands in regard to the way things are, the "law" of this age (*saeculum*) and the suffering it engenders. The cross announces the end of this *saeculum* and empowers one to live it out here and now.

Reading the cross in an epistemological key offers the invitation to move constantly to the margins of the text, to the frame of picture that is normally all too familiar and seek what Foucault called "subjugated knowledges," the knowledges that stand at the edge of the established canonic epistemes, the conventionally accepted régimes of truth.[29] The cross calls for this, attested to by the fact that a scandal of enormous magnitude, a foolishness so easy to sidestep, became the cornerstone of the Christian faith.

The criticism of this interpretation is easy to anticipate. If this reading is correct, then anything goes and no norms are left, the criticism would say. The response is twofold. First, a centripetal force is pulling toward the core of biblical and historical frames by their sheer traditional density; that is, even if we move to the frames (plural, since there are many traditions) we do so because we have originally been framed. We never start *tabula rasa*, we already inhabit a given frame of meaning so dense that it will never allow for sheer arbitrariness. Second, and most important, the eschatological criterion presented above must be understood in the context of the apocalyptic movement within which Christianity first found and expressed itself. This apocalyptic criterion suggests that the *eschata* be interpreted as the point where the last and the first meet each other in its manifold sense: temporal and spatial, but also social

Peter dislikes the ways of the world that the cross epitomizes, but loves God who is assumed to do away with the ways of the world. The dissonance comes in the moment in which Peter becomes aware that God chooses the cross.

[29] Michel Foucault, *Power and Knowledge: Selected Interviews and Other Writings: 1972–1977*, ed. Colin Gordon (New York: Pantheon, 1980), 82.

and psychological. This is what leads us to the discussion of reading the cross from the "standpoint of the subjugated."[30] South African theologian Simon Maimela reminds us, and pertinently so, that even a theology of the cross must ask to whom it speaks and who is the speaker.[31]

[30] Donna Haraway quoted in Solberg, *Compelling Knowledge*, 42.

[31] Simon Maimela, "The Suffering of Human Divisions and the Cross," in *The Scandal of a Crucified World: Perspectives on the Cross and Suffering*, ed. Yacob Tesfai (Maryknoll, N.Y.: Orbis, 1994), 37f.

Cross and Poetry

The Mask of God and Human Accountability toward Creation

6

Why was Christ EXPOSED on the Cross?
Pier Paolo Pasolini

If the cross of Christ refashions our knowledge, our perception of the world, and even in some sense condemns our world, what does an authentic theology of the cross reveal about our world? In the light of the cross, can we understand the material world—its systems, ecology, and its destiny—in a new way?

Cross and Creation: A Contradiction?

Is a theology of the cross inherently environmentally unfriendly? The cross spells judgment, the judgment of the world. Flesh comes to a languid end. Another world, not this one, is left only as a dim light of hope, not any brighter than those few words promised by Jesus to the fellow convict dying at his side: "Truly, I say to you, today you will be with me in paradise" (Luke 23:42). The promise of the kingdom comes as a condemnation of this world. It seems to be forgotten that this indictment refers to the existing sociopolitical and religious order of things, not to the whole of creation. Thus, theologians who are sympathetic to the message of the cross often disparage concerns about creation and ecology, considering them as diversions that take attention away from the pressing issues of the day.

Gustavo Gutiérrez, the first internationally acclaimed liberation theologian, in his early manifesto of 1971, *A Theology of Liberation*, decried the discourse of "theologians of the developed world." Their concern with questions about creation reflected a political naïveté that had "sapped most of their energy" to fight the causes at hand.[1] The counter-criticism is expected; a theology so concerned with an apocalyptic turn of events is bound to scold not only the "order" of this world but the created world as such, nature as a whole.

The claim attributed to Luther, that if he knew that the world soon would end he still would plant an apple tree, is little consolation for the massive amount of theology invested in the cross were the cross viewed only as the tragic overcoming of a creation that has gone astray and not as a radical affirmation of the incarnation of God. If the case, as discussed earlier, is God against God, does this imply a license for anything else? Is this a way of rephrasing the Latin dictum "Justice be done even if the world is doomed" (*fiat iustitia et pereat mundus*) to "let God be God even if the world is trashed?"

These criticisms are as old as environmental awareness, which emerged half a century ago. In 1967 Lynn White Jr. wrote "The Historical Roots of Our Ecological Crisis," charging the Western Judeo-Christian tradition with an endemically malignant attitude toward nature.[2] The article started a fire in a theological circus overly concerned with keeping the christological performance in the center ring. Although theology of the cross was not directly implicated in accusations against Western theology, bringing it up only added fuel to the flames. In any case, the message pointed directly to Christology as fertilizer feeding the parasitical roots of the ecological crisis. Theology in the West, too much concerned about the relationship between human depravity and God's saving message, had

---

[1] Gustavo Gutiérrez, *A Theology of Liberation* (Maryknoll, N.Y.: Orbis Books, 1973), 173. See, as a defense of a theology of creation within a liberation frame, Vítor Westhelle, "Creation Motifs in Search of a Vital Space," in *Lift Every Voice: Constructing Christian Theologies from the Underside*, ed. Susan B. Thistlethwaite and Mary Potter Engel (Maryknoll, N.Y.: Orbis Books, 1998), 146–58.

[2] Lynn White, Jr., "The Historical Roots of Our Ecological Crisis," *Science* 155 (1967): 1203–07.

lost a more incisive view of nature. Theology had superseded nature with the supernatural. The cross was implied in this firestorm, interpreted as a "crossing" from the natural to the supernatural.

A theocentric perspective in theology followed the criticism. H. Richard Niebuhr called twentieth-century theology "Unitarianism of the Second Article."[3] Others followed suit and began to exercise the muscles of an atrophied doctrine of creation in view of the ecological challenge. Proposals ranged from renewal of Thomistic infrastructural approaches to nature (as the positive foundation for the supernatural), to quasi-pantheistic views of nature and creation as "original blessing"[4] or as the divine mother Earth raped by her own children.

Theology of the Word, prominent in neoorthodox Protestant theology, also prompted the resurgence of a tamer creation theology with different characteristics. As opposed to the Roman Catholic-inspired tendency to regard nature as positive information for the construction of the relationship between Creator and creature, Protestants favored a "negative" epistemological approach. The theology of the Word insisted on creation not as a basis for redemption but as the "first act of salvation" (Karl Barth). Still, the negativity of the cross, its alleged negation of the world, looms large and in this Luther's theology of the cross is implicated. Nevertheless, it is important to stress that Luther has a different attitude from the infrastructural or neoorthodox approaches to the issue.

In spite of the Reformer's strong emphasis on the theology of creation, his followers have been reticent, at least in modern times, to follow his lead. With the exception of a few major works in the last century,[5] Luther's

---

[3] See James Gustafson, *Ethics from a Theocentric Perspective: Theology and Ethics* (Chicago: University of Chicago Press, 1981), 53–56.

[4] Matthew Fox, *Original Blessing* (New York: Penguin, 2000).

[5] In recent times significant work has been done in this area, but until then significant contributions are few. Among these are: Philip S. Watson, *Let God be God! An Interpretation of the Theology of Martin Luther* (Philadelphia: Muhlenberg Press, 1948); Regin Prenter, *Schöpfung und Erlösung: Dogmatik* (Göttingen: Vandenhoeck & Ruprecht, 1958–60); Joseph A. Sittler, "Called to Unity," *Ecumenical Review* 14 (1962): 177–87; David Löfgren, *Die Theologie der Schöpfung bei Luther* (Göttingen: Vandenhoeck & Ruprecht, 1960); Kjell Ove Nilsson, *Simul: Das Miteinander von Göttlichem und Menschlichem Luthers Theologie* (Göttingen: Vandenhoeck & Ruprecht, 1966); and, more recently, Oswald Bayer, *Shöpfung als Anrede: Zu einer Hermeneutik der Schöpfung* (Tübingen: J.C.B. Mohr, 1990).

emphasis on creation has been filtered through the theology of divinely instituted orders of creation (*Ordnungstheologie*), a static view of nature allied to political and ideological embarrassments like support of German Nazism. Luther's concern with creation was dismissed as a well-intended gesture, even an insightful inventory of sparse theological motifs, but not fit for a systematic and foundational theological argument.

The point of dispute is the difficulty in linking Luther's theology of the cross (asserting that "God is not to be found but in suffering and in the cross"[6]) with theology of creation (and Luther's affirmation of *duplex cognitio Dei*—the "double knowledge of God"[7]). Even the distinction between special and general revelation as a way of interpreting Luther's double knowledge of God has been regarded with suspicion by those who consider the cross as the radical and the only specific feature of his theology: *crux sola nostra theologia*.[8]

Some regard restricting God's revelation to a Christian *specificum* a hindrance to growing awareness of ethnic, cultural, and religious pluralism or to the ecological sensitivies of those eager to read the divine hieroglyphics in the book of nature. Are these incompatible ways of organizing a theology? Are a theology of creation and a theology of the cross intrinsically at odds? A close examination of the theology of the cross in distinction to the infrastructural and the neoorthodox perspectives can be an inspiring source for a theology that is sensitive to environmental concerns.

The Tortured Flesh of God

Let us consider these questions, with regard to the distinctions presented earlier between the visible and the Word (audible), between creature and Creator, the outer and the inner, between what the senses perceive and what grace reveals to the heart. In spite of these suspicious binarisms, the distinctions have a heuristic value that helps more in tacking up the issue than appealing head-on to a dogmatic differentiation between the

---

[6] *At Deum non inveniri nisi in passionibus et crucem. WA* 1, 362, 28f.

[7] *Duplex est cognition Dei, WA* 40/I, 607, 28.

[8] *WA* 5, 217, 2–3.

first and the second articles of faith, between creation and redemption. Before it becomes a dogmatic issue of relating creation and redemption, it is indeed an epistemological problem. At the epistemological level, those binarisms will question their own ontological validity. When one examines the procedures by which the binary distinctions between right and left, correct and wrong, are established, the dismantling of their classificatory power has begun and their erosion sets in.

There is a paradoxical and asymmetrical relation between the two terms of the binary distinctions by which Luther works to formulate his understanding of the double knowledge. "Paradoxical" means that one (the visible) points to the other (the Word) but is in it simultaneously contradicted, while the latter becomes visible in the former yet in a dissimulated or masked way. "Asymmetry" means that what appears on one side of the binary categories is not mirrored in the other but is shaped in it—or perhaps by it—in unexpected ways. This argumentative devise is called irony: a rejection of analogical reasoning with apparent analogical correspondence.

In Luther's writings, particularly in his commentaries on the Psalms, Luther affirms that nature is full of parables, metaphors, and signs—even sermons better than the ones preached in many churches. Nevertheless, he would deny that the Creator as such, or the Redeemer, can be known through our native faculties. What is seen is debased if it is not seen through faith. Only faith can see creation![9] The view we have of *nature* is the blindness we have to *creation*. Analogical correspondence between these two is truncated. The "mechanism" through which we link creation and Creator cannot be grasped externally, because we are implicated in it through and through; we cannot observe it from a transcendent standpoint (*sub species aeternitatis*).

The famous metaphor of nature as a mask (*larva*) or wrapping (*involucrum*) of God lifts up this sense of being implicated. Humans, as God's creatures, are God's masks through which we observe, experience, and interact with God's masks in creation in general. We are masks

---

[9] *WA* 38, 53, 24f.

interacting with nature's masks? To understand this we need to go back to the mask metaphor in Luther's writings. Luther did not adopt the mask motif from the Greek theatre, but from the medieval carnival. In these festivities the mask served as means of caricaturing reality, revealing it but, at the same time, concealing it in its reverse. The mask presented popular projections of social, religious, and political life with burlesque resources within the space of the festival. Confined in that space, it also concealed the true social relations of everyday life: it provided a glimpse of the "unseen" hidden social system and intentionally distorted it. Nature as a mask, following this metaphor taken from the carnival, is the carnival of creation in which we as masks are a part.[10]

The same goes also for the closely associated wrapping motif: it reveals a presence while denying to our eyes' sight any evidence of its content, or even its existence. Consider a nicely wrapped present one receives. The wrapping is beautiful to see, but it also conceals what is essential, the gift it holds wrapped. One who receives a wrapped present knows of the promising existence of the package's unseen content only by trust in the giver (for it could be a practical joke or a bomb sent anonymously through the mail).

The visible things (*visibilia*) do not allow for any direct or even indirect access to revelation (except in Barth's sense of double indirectness[11]), but they make it present simultaneously directly and indirectly. In the visible presence God is a "mediated immediacy."[12] Yet this very affirmation attests only to God's utter absence. To rely on natural reason for the indications of God's presence will reveal only the idol of the heart (*idolum cordis*).[13] The visible becomes an idol if it is seen as a directly reflected image of the unseen, when the gaze of the beholder is captivated, arrested by it. In the words of Jean-Luc Marion, "the idol shows what it sees. It shows that

---

[10] For a comprehensive analysis of the medieval carnival and the role of the mask during late Middle Ages into the time of Luther, it is a must to read Mikhail Bakhtin, *A Cultura Popular na Idade Média e no Renascimento* (São Paulo: Huicitec, 1987).

[11] Karl Barth, *Die kirchliche Dogmatik* I/1 (Zürich: Zollikon, 1952), 173–80.

[12] *See* John Baillie, *God Was In Christ: An Essay on Incarnation and Atonement* (New York: Charles Scribner, 1948).

[13] *WA* 14, 587, 30.

which, indeed, occupies the field of the visible....It freezes in a figure that which vision aims at in a glance."[14]

At the same time it can become an icon of the unseen if the gaze does not stop at and is not frozen by what is presented to sight, even if it cannot go beyond it to have a direct vision of the unseen. Again, in the words of Marion, "the icon alone offers an open face, because it opens in itself the visible onto the invisible, by offering its spectacle to be transgressed—not to be seen, but to be venerated."[15] An oxymoron, as in "mirroring transparency," might convey the meaning intended here. What is reflected is not the visible presence as such, as the reflection in a mirror, but it is an absence *manifested* in the reflection: a specter, should it be called? It is akin to looking in a mirror and seeing through our appearances what we "really" are. The specter is not in the image, but in the aura of what it hides.

Nevertheless, this does not mean that the visible is indifferent or neutral with regard to the knowledge of God. The *Deus vestitus*, the clothed God (another of Luther's metaphors), might be the potential idol, but it protects us from the *Deus nudus*, the naked God, which is the irresistible abyss. The clothed God is the representation of that which cannot be represented. By affirming its very absence it simultaneously offers the experience of presence. The clothed God is the God of religious experiences in which humans open themselves to whatever transcends real existence while, at the same time, closing themselves to the radical experience of otherness. Philosopher and political thinker Cornelius Castoriadis offers a pertinent commentary.

> Religion offers a name to the unnamable, a representation to that which cannot be represented, a place to that which cannot be located. It actualizes and satisfies, at the same time, the experience of the Abyss and the refusal to accept it, circumscribing it—pretending to circumscribe it—giving it one or many figures, assigning it the places it dwells, the moments it privileges, the people who embody it, the words and texts that reveal it. Religion is, par excellence, the representation/concealment of Chaos. It constitutes a *compromise* that prepares at the same time the

---

[14] Jan-Luc Marion, *God without Being* (Chicago: University of Chicago Press, 1991), 26.
[15] See ibid., 19.

impossibility for human beings closing themselves in the here-and-now of their "real existence" and their almost equal impossibility in accepting the experience of the Abyss.[16]

This compromise is the visible in which we invest so much, the material world that can be both an idol as well the iconic wrapping of the divine.[17] Such is the importance of what Luther called the "majesty of matter:"[18] it prevents direct accessibility to divine revelation in order to convince us of the need for God's self-revelation through the Word. In this sense the double knowledge of God is affirmed, even in paradoxical and asymmetric terms. What Luther said in his introduction to the German Mass (1526), about the efficacy of the liturgical elements, is exactly what could be said about the visible in general: not because of them, but never without them.[19] What the Reformer said in theses 19-20 of the Heidelberg Disputation[20] is relevant: God is neither to be seen or sought behind creation, nor be inferred from it, but only recognized in and through it. This "in and through" is misleading, however, if we do not understand that creation "reveals" the concealment, the absence of God, our own blindness to the divine reality.

Knowledge *sub species crucis*

Behind the notion of the *Deus absconditus,* the hidden God, lies the conviction that the visible in general presents to us a clothed God, who as such remains a mystery. The *Deus absconditus* is not to be taken as a speculative argument that claims to know God through the evil we

---

[16] Cornelius Castoriadis, *Os Destinos do Totalitarismo e outros Escritos* (Porto Alegre: LPM, 1985), 113.

[17] See Vítor Westhelle, "Wrappings of the Divine: Location and Vocation in Theological Perspective," *Currents in Theology and Mission* 31, no. 5 (October 2004): 368–80.

[18] *WA* 39/II, 4, 32.

[19] *WA* 19, 72–73.

[20] "That person does not deserve to be called a theologian who looks upon the invisible things of God as though they were clearly perceptible in those things which have actually happened. He deserves to be called a theologian, however, who comprehends the visible and manifest things of God seen through suffering and the cross," Martin Luther, "Heidelberg Disputation (1518)," *Luther's Works* vol. 31 *Career of the Reformer I*, ed. and trans. Harold J. Grimm (Philadelphia: Fortress, 1957), 40.

experience as the alien work of God (*opus alienum*). The rejection of this argument was given earlier. God is not only hidden in wrath and evil, but in external things in general. The concealment of God is realized in God's wrath through the *opus alienum* only because through evil, in particular, we become aware that the visible does not reveal God, certainly not as an epiphany. This means that God is hidden in beauty and goodness of nature as much as in ugliness and evil. The point is that it is tempting to find and rely on evidences of the divine in goodness and beauty while simultaneously rejecting evil as a pedagogue. In other words, beauty suggests a univocal epiphany, a direct manifestation of God. This leads to idolatry. Not because beauty and goodness are false instructors, but because they arrest our gaze and blind us to suffering and evil. The goodness I see conceals an evil that is displayed outside the field of my vision. And the reverse is also true: the evil I encounter conceals the goodness that is hidden to the sight. In other words, as much as goodness and beauty, evil and hideousness are not beyond God's infinity.

In this sense, there is only an epistemological (not a logical, let alone ontological) primacy of the *opus alienum* in the knowledge of God for theology. God should not be praised for the greatness of creation in spite of evil; God should be praised in the midst of evil where God's continuing creation works out of the annihilating force of evil. Because of this force, the nihility of evil, God's creativity is made manifest. It is this creativity, then, and not evil itself, that makes the knowledge of God possible. This is the fundamental thesis for supporting theologically the *creatio ex nihilo*, the creation out of nothing, out of sin and evil, the terrifying abyss of utter emptiness, the *horror vacui*.

A call for responsibility grows out of the awareness of our sinful condition. Nature as such did not fall but suffers the curse of evil because of human fault. For Luther this becomes a sermon about our condition as destroyers of creation. "Not only in churches, therefore, do we hear ourselves charged with sin. All the fields, yes almost the entire creation is full of such sermons, reminding us of our sin."[21] Therefore, the point in Luther's use of the mask motif is not so much to stress that God is

[21] *WA* 42, 156, 24–25.

hidden, as to underscore that we are hiding ourselves by not recognizing this mask for what it is, either by speculating from its appearance the face behind it, or simply by ignoring it.

The hidden God raises a mask by which the humans might recognize themselves as in a deceptive mirror. Humans are called to recognize themselves in its beauty and in its sinister appearance. The *Deus absconditus* is the *Deus revelatus* because God's concealment, once recognized, prompts the emergence of the *homo revelatus*, the human revealed for what the human really is. The Reformation's appeal for letting God be God corresponds to the motto "let nature [human included] be nature." Auschwitz, Hiroshima, and the holes in the ozone layer are the masks of God raised for our self-recognition. By them we measure ourselves as much as by the lilies in the fields. In the evil we experience, however, we have a fissured mask in whose cracks we have the terrible sight of the abyss of emptiness. This is why evil, as a fissured mask, becomes a pedagogue: through its cracks we know that behind it there is no pretty face to behold. Through these cracks the Word that convicts us resounds as does the promise of restoration.

Poetry, God, and Humans

If the visible is the projection of our inner beauty and hideousness, the Word is always the word of the other. If I can possess what I see (because I can reduce it conceptually to my sameness), the Word comes always from beyond the limits of my possible domain. Without the Word, reality loses all focus and telos, for the visible is that which is not transparent, it does not allow for transcendence; it is by definition the immanent. In keeping the metaphor of the fissured mask, when the visible allows for transcendence, for the otherness to break through, it does it by the horrendous emptiness that the cracks expose. Yet in so doing the Word is the creative force in God's continuous work of creation. As the transcendent force capable of bringing reality out of nonexisting things (*creatio ex nihilo*), the Word calls for the mending and restoration of the cracks, recreating reality.

The Word can only be the way in which otherness comes to me, however, if I have accepted the visible for what it is, named things for what they are. To ignore the visible or to flee from it in search of the pure Word is to take the cross out of this world, something like what we have in Salvador Dali's paintings of the crucifixion. Dali reveals with sarcasm how we have sublimated the cross.[22] This is but another version of the "theology of glory." The difference is that the one Luther criticized took the visible as a mediation to the invisible, while in this case it is a direct or immediate leap, a *rapture* into the invisible, not realizing that the invisible—encompassed in the visible—is the very transparency of the visible. The visible without the Word is blind, the Word without the visible is empty.

Suffering, the unbearable sight of the visible, makes the visible transparent when the suffering seen is proclaimed by the Word to be the suffering for which humans share responsibility, either by action that perpetrates it or by omission in failing to respond to it. The cross of Christ, the archetypical shape suffering takes in the Christian story, manifests the *Deus revelatus* when we consider it to be the suffering of God's own self, for which we are truly responsible. The confession of the centurion in Mark 15:39 is of such theological significance not because he knew the deeds or the teachings of Jesus (most likely he did not), but because he knew himself to be part of all of us who directly or indirectly imposed that suffering. Seeing himself in that mask became for the centurion that "mirroring transparency" into his own condition. He knew himself at the moment he recognized God, and he recognized God because he came to know who he was.

In the cross of Christ general and particular revelation come together, for God's creativity is witnessed when the annihilating force of the emptiness of the abyss is made manifest. The cross is the material criterion by which the visible becomes constitutive for the knowledge of God; the theology of creation is the formal criterion for the recognition of God's

---

[22] These paintings are a radical indictment of the Christian sublimated use of the cross. The very popularity of copies of the paintings among Christians results from the trap Dali set to catch Christians in their glorification of the cross.

revelation as creation out of nothing, that is, evil and suffering in general. In other words, through the theology of creation we know that the cross of Christ is formally identical with the suffering of the world; through the theology of the cross the suffering in and of the world is recognized as the locus of God's creative work.

The suffering of nature (human included) assumes a privileged epistemological status because divine creativity manifests itself in and through it. The primacy of the Word directs the gaze and calls attention to suffering as the site of God's present activity. On the human side the response is one of creating, after the image humans inherited from God the Creator, producing a reality through which glory is given to whom it is due. This work is not meritorious precisely because it takes the form of a doxology, as Article XX of the Augsburg Confession states: "It is taught among us that good works should and must be done, not that we are to rely on them to have grace but that we may do God's will and glorify him." Nothing can render to God greater glory than to be God's cooperators in the care and stewardship of this world. The expression *cooperation* to designate the human partnership with God in the work of the worldly régime was used by Luther himself in the "Bondage of the Will," in which he distinguishes the labor of God, who creates out of nothing and out of nothing saves, and the work we do in preserving and sustaining the gift of creation as it was given to us: God "does not work without us, because it is for this very thing he has recreated and preserves us, that he might work in us and we might cooperate with him. Thus it is through us that he preaches, shows mercy to the poor, comforts the afflicted."[23]

---

[23] *See* Martin Luther, "The Bondage of the Will," *Luther's Works* vol. 33 *Career of the Reformer III*, ed. Philip S. Watson (Philadelphia: Fortress, 1972), 243. A novel and very relevant effort to convey this idea of cooperation with God while maintaining the infinite difference between the creator and creation is offered by Philip Hefner's concept of the "created co-creator." See his *The Human Factor: Evolution, Culture, and Religion* (Minneapolis: Fortress Press, 1993). For a critical discussion of the concept see Vítor Westhelle, "The Poet, the Practitioner and the Beholder," *Zygon: Journal of Religion and Science* 39, no. 4 (2004): 748–50; and Philip Hefner, "Can the Created Co-Creator be Lutheran? A Response to Svend Andersen," *Dialog: A Journal of Theology* 44, no. 2 (Summer 2005): 184–88.

The difference between God's work and our labor is that our endeavor will never bring something out of nothingness. God alone does that. By virtue of being endowed with the image of God, what we can do is to produce simulacra of divine artistry by working on a mask that God has given us, even though it is now cracked by our sin. Human *poietics* is derivative. Humans are poets of a medieval carnival mending masks through which they protect themselves from the terrible sight of the abyss, the vision of the *Deus nudus*, the *horror vacui*. This poetic work, after the image of God, "the poet of heaven and earth" (*poietes ouranou tes ges*), as the Nicene Creed confesses, is our ecological responsibility in all the dimensions of our existence in the earthly régime: in politics, home, civil society, economy, and church. Yet this work also produces idols to which hearts and minds will cling, as Luther described in the commentary to the First Commandment in the Large Catechism as the root cause of either true faith or of idolatry.

God Exposed

Ecological responsibility, thus, is neither a mystical or romantic response to the positive goodness of creation, nor conformity to a "natural law," but a doxological act of repentance and renewal out of the depth, out of the void that threatens us from the cracks of a fissured mask. We should not fear that nature has become artificial (Karl Marx); we should fear a view of nature, bucolic or scientific, that veers us away from the experience of suffering and the cross. Far from a naïve view of nature or from a modern divorce between *homo* and *natura*, Luther's theology provides criteria for facing evil in nature and society: the visibility of suffering in the silence of the innocent opens up the space in which the creative Word resonates. Luther is only a commentary, not the text, but a commentary on a text, on an anti-poem that is God's exposed nakedness on the tree of execration, creation (*poiesis*) in its reverse: destruction, down to its essential, the human hanging on a cross.

Yet in this shadowy exposure to the languor of the flesh, to this courage to leave the flesh but to endure it to the ultimate consequences, revelation is consumed, in the sense of being finished and also of reaching its fulfillment. This radical immanentism of God's own self in creation defies with embodiment the powers that work to bring the "poem" of God to naught.

With the incarnation, God the poet becomes a poem and takes up the mask that is creation; with the cross, the poem (creation) fades while exposed to our gaze, and God eclipses like the sun in the middle of the day. Do we evade the sight? Do we sublimate it? This was done to God then and it is done today: an assault on the integrity of the majesty of matter.

Italian writer and film director Pier Paolo Pasolini expressed this in a poem with disarming force.

> All his wounds are open to the sun
> and He dies under the eyes
> of everyone: even His mother
> under His breast, belly and knees,
> watches His body suffer.
> Dawn and dusk cast light
> on His open arms and April
> softens His exhibition of death
> to gazes that burn Him.
> Why was Christ EXPOSED on the Cross?
> Oh, the heart shudders at the naked
> body of the youth…atrocious
> offence to its raw modesty…
> The sun and the gazes!
> You must expose yourself (is this what the
> poor nailed-up Christ teaches?),
> the clarity of the heart is worthy
> of every sneer, every sin,
> every more naked passion…
> (is this what the Crucifix means?
> sacrifice every day the gift
> renounce every day forgiveness
> cast yourself ingenuous over the abyss).

We will be offered on the cross,
on the pillory, between the pupils
limpid with ferocious joy,
leaving open to irony the drops
of blood from the breast to the knees,
gentle and ridiculous, trembling
with intellect and passion in the play
of the heart burning from its fire,
testifying to the scandal.[24]

Michael Hardt's commentary on this poem should not be paraphrased.

Take me now! Pasolini is fascinated with the immodest offering of Christ's body on the cross. His wounds are open. His entire body—breast, belly, sex, and knees—are burning under the gaze of the crowd and elements. At the point of death, Christ is all body, an open piece of flesh, abandoned, exposed. This is when Christ's emptied divinity, its radiant surfaces shine forth most brightly.... Erotic exposure, paradoxically, does not really involve seeing and being seen. In fact, exposure subverts a certain regime of vision. The exposed self does not reveal a secret self that had been hidden, but rather dissolves any self that could be apprehended. We not only have nothing left to hide, we no longer present any separate thing for the eyes to grasp. We become imperceptible.[25]

The exposure is the scandal. Why would the Christ not die of old age quietly in his bed? The question suggests the answer: in the cross we know that we can no longer remain imperceptible. How convenient is it to hide the wounds open and displayed for the gaze?

---

[24] Cited by Michael Hardt, "Exposure: Pasolini in the Flesh," in Brian Massumi, ed., *A Shock to Thought: Expression after Deleuze and Guattari* (London: Routledge, 2002), 77–78.
[25] Ibid., 80.

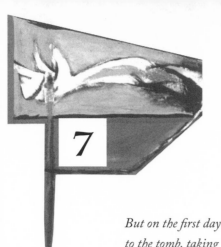

The Practice of Resurrection
On Asserting the Openness
of Past Victimizations

*But on the first day of the week, at early dawn, they came
to the tomb, taking the spices that they had prepared.*

Luke 24:1

Suppose a group of earnest Christian laymen were taken prisoner and
set down in a desert without an episcopally ordained priest among them.
And suppose that they were to come to a common mind there and then
in the desert and elect one among them, whether he were married or not,
and charge him to baptize, say mass, pronounce absolution, and preach
the gospel. Such man would be as truly a priest as though he had been
ordained by all the bishops and popes in the world.[1]

In this passage of his "Letter to the Christian Nobility" Luther invites a
comparison between the context in which the Reformation came about
and that wilderness where stranded people had to find a way of carving
out their own freedom, of charting a space of possibilities; the Reformation was an uncharted "territory." He also claims the right of people
under those conditions to find their own legitimate way of organizing

---

[1] Martin Luther, "To the Christian Nobility of the German Nation Concerning the Reform of
the Christian Estate (1520)," *Luther's Works* vol. 44 *The Christian in Society I*, ed. and rev. James
Atkinson, trans. Charles M. Jacobs (Philadelphia: Fortress, 1966), 128.

themselves, without the necessary sanction of the ecclesial and political establishment. But on what grounds does he make this claim?

He was not advancing a defense of human autonomy as it would be put forward during the Enlightenment. His example appeals not for a right to anarchy but to an insurgent right to claim with legitimacy the very powers that the hierarchical ecclesial system of his day had organized within orders of privilege. Those in the hierarchy self-entrusted themselves with the deposit of the revelation, which supposedly contained the available and inerrant knowledge of the divine.

Luther seeks no exception to the rule for this hypothetical group, as if to say: "In spite of the irregular conditions we should recognize them as having established a legitimate office." Instead, he vindicates a radical catholicity that exceeds that of those who claimed to administer it. The man chosen to be a priest in the imaginary group is not merely an acceptable exception to the rule, he is "truly a priest as though he has been ordained by *all the bishops* and *popes*." Such ironic gestures are characteristic of the Reformer: a group set apart and thus defined as heretical (for heresy means to be set apart) has more legitimacy than what is considered to be the rule and the norm; values are subverted.

Finally, the image of displacement as an opening for the *new* formation to come about suggests that this new (the *novum* that the West has so often projected into the future[2]) might in fact be some*where* else. Western utopian thinking, which translates the no-place (*u-topos*) into a future time to come, is moved in Luther's spatial imagery to another-place (*heterotopia*). If we think of the eschatological vision as another world that comes about, this other world might be the very world of the other, the one who is different and excluded from our world.

What frames such a vision is the eschatological ethos, an understanding of revelation that both knows the end and owns it and also becomes a place for a beginning. This eschatology, what Walter Benjamin called "Messianic gate,"[3] represents for the powers (that be) the unthinkable limit, but are for those who inhabit it, those who are at the limit, the

---

[2] Robert Nisbet, *History of the Idea of Progress* (New York: Basic Books, 1979).

[3] Walter Benjamin, *Illuminations*, ed. Hannah Arendt (New York: Schocken, 1969), 264.

medium in which condemnation is experienced and yet only there is liberation a possibility. Condemnation and liberation meet at that liminal moment that is at the same time a "limit-to" (to the edges of our world) and also a "limit-of" (of a world to come).[4] The poet Friedrich Hölderlin expressed it this way: "Near is God, but where danger lies, grows also that which saves."[5] United by the experience of liminality, both the Reformation and movements inspired by liberation theologies are committed to a reorientation of the whole theological endeavor. This is expressed in the famous definition of Luther: the cross alone is our theology (*crux sola est nostra theologia*).[6]

The radical importance of such an expression is that it makes plain that it is neither a theology among others nor a doctrine but a way of doing theology; it does not cancel any other theology but brings a provoking, ironic gesture.[7] It is a way of recognizing the other and hidden side of history, the margins, the excluded, the stranded ones, the "crucified people" (Ignacio Ellacuría), the "nonpersons" (Gustavo Gutiérrez) as the privileged space of God's self-revelation.

In the theses for the Heidelberg Disputation, we read:

19. That person does not deserve to be called a theologian who looks upon the invisible things of God as though they were clearly perceptible in those things which have actually happened.
20. He deserves to be called a theologian, however, who comprehends the visible and manifest things [*posteriora*] of God seen through suffering and the cross.

---

[4] For the theological definition and usage of these categories, see David Tracy, *Blessed Rage for Order: The New Pluralism in Theology* (New York: Seabury, 1975), 92–94.

[5] Friedrich Hölderlin, *Gedichte-Hyperion* (Augsburg: Wilhelm Goldmann, 1978), 138.

[6] *WA* 5, 176, 32–33.

[7] Luther preferred to use the expression "theologian of the cross" instead of "theology of the cross" in order to lift up the fact that such a theology is a praxis and not a doctrinal locus. One could also say that for Luther "theology of the cross," *theologia crucis*, is to be read primarily as a subjective genitive, as a theology done from the perspective of the cross, and not a theology about the cross, which would be the objective sense of the genitive. See Gerhard Forde, *On Being a Theologian of the Cross: Reflections on Luther's Heidelberg Disputation, 1518* (Grand Rapids: Eerdmans, 1997), 70–71.

21. A theologian of glory calls evil good and good evil. The theologian of the cross calls the thing what it actually is. This is clear: He who does not know Christ does not know God hidden in suffering....[8]

Luther's indictment of the theology of his day was also a critique of the theories of the cross, either ontological or moral, in the plea for a theology that is a practice of passion (*usus passionis*), an engaging experience and an intentional disposition.[9] As such, the cross becomes an epistemological locus, the privileged place of God's own self-revelation; it is more than a past event in which atonement was accomplished or a moral example for a virtuous life. Before Luther named it a theology of the cross, *theologia crucis*, the motif was clearly presented by Paul in 1 Corinthians 1, where he calls the message of the cross a scandal (*skandalon*), foolishness (*moria*), and weakness (*asthenes*); a message about life found in death, a message of liberation that can only be seen through the lens of oppression, a message about God hidden in the mask of a devil, a message about goodness that can only shine when evil is named for what it is. Maximus the Confessor (seventh century), a forerunner of the "theology of the cross," put it this way:

The more [God] becomes comprehensible through [Incarnation], so much more through it is he known to be incomprehensible. For he is hidden...in his revelation. And this mystery of Jesus in itself remains hidden, and can be drawn out by no reason, by no intellect, but when spoken of it remains ineffable, and when understood unknown. What could do more to demonstrate the proof of the divine transcendence of being than this: revelation shows that it is hidden, reason that it is unspeakable, and intellect that it is transcendentally unknowable, and further, its assumption of being that it is beyond being.[10]

---

[8] Martin Luther, "Heidelberg Disputation (1518)," *Luther's Works* vol. 31 *Career of the Reformer I*, ed. and trans. Harold J. Grimm (Philadelphia: Fortress, 1957), 40.

[9] *Es ist eyn unterscheyd praedicare passionem Christi et usus passionis. Diabolus primium eciam praedicat, secundum vero spiritussanctus tantum. WA* 17 I, 71, 26–28.

[10] "Difficulty 5," in Andrew Louth, ed., trans., and commentary, *Maximus the Confessor* (London: Routledge, 1996), 173.

And even more sharply:

> The Lord, who wanted us to understand that we should not look for natural necessity in what is above nature, wanted to bring about his work by means of opposites. He therefore fulfilled his life by death and accomplished his glory by means of dishonour.[11]

This perspective recognizes what Latin American theologians have called the "battle of gods"[12]—in such experiences no theoretical or orthodox discernment can be made about who the real God is. In this sense we read Luther's statement that "God cannot be God unless He becomes a devil; and the devil will not be the devil before being God."[13] "Orthopraxis" is the word for this methodological approach, which was for Luther the way of the theologian of the cross. Better to call it a practice of solidarity with the pain of the world, which follows the encounter with Christ crucified.

We are unable to decide whether we serve God or the devil unless our position or perspective, our location, is that of cross and suffering. Hence the revelation of God—that which God allows us to see—is doubly elusive. It is indirect in that God's self-revelation is given through means other than the divine (it is not an epiphany) and it is doubly so when it appears contrary to what is divine. The ironic gesture keeps coming back. Karl Barth calls it a double indirectness in his reading of Luther's notion of "revelation hidden under its opposite" (*revelatio sub contraria specie*). According to Barth, "the nerve of Luther's thought is that the *larva Dei* [mask of God], the indirectness of his self-communication, is a double one issued not only through its created character, but also through the sinfulness of the creature."[14]

---

[11] Cited by Yves Congar, *I Believe in the Holy Spirit*, 3 vols. (New York: Crossroad, 1983), 3:15.

[12] Pablo Richard et al., *La lucha de los dioses: los ídolos de la opresión y la búsqueda del Dios liberador* (San José/Managua: DEI/CAV, 1980).

[13] Martin Luther, "Psalm 117," *Luther's Works* vol. 14 *Selected Psalms III*, ed. Jaroslav Pelikan, trans. Edward Sittler (St. Louis: Concordia, 1958), 31.

[14] Karl Barth, *Die kirchliche Dogmatik* I/1 (Zürich: Evangelischer Verlag Zillokon, 1952), 173–74.

"Were You There when They Crucified My Lord?"

The distinction between theology of the cross as a theory and theology of the cross as a practice can now be elucidated. "Theory" might be in the moral sense, as an example to be followed, or in the ontological sense, which describes an event between God and sinful humanity. "Practice" (*usus*) is not to be understood only as an action or operation, but also a disposition or a *habitus* in the sense that it entails, more than action, also an involvement in the midst of the circumstances in which the practice takes place. It is a dispositional practice exemplified by the expression *theologia crucis*. There is a difference between the subjective and the objective sense of the genitive in the expression. Luther used the expression "theologian of the cross," instead of "theology of the cross," indicating his preference for theology done from the point of view or perspective of the cross, as a disposition, rather than theology *about* the cross.

What allows us to establish this distinction is our *position*, our location vis-à-vis the cross out of which we *dis-pose*. "Were you there when they crucified my Lord?" The question of the old spiritual implies, as Kierkegaard did, that we can be contemporaneous with Jesus, that we can be there where God is being crucified, even today. "Were you there?" The question can go even further to ask our location in relationship to the cross. This location establishes whether we are theologians of the cross or theologians of glory. Different circumstances and contexts establish different narratives, different possibilities to theologize.

Luther's distinction between the theologian of the cross and the theologian of glory has become a commonplace and too narrow a typology to account for the subtle ways in which we relate to the cross. I will use four different possibilities, producing four theological voices, to illustrate my point. Typologies, even expanded ones, are simplifications, even oversimplifications. They don't account for the complexities of real-life situations, but they can help us to discern distinct courses of action, to signal possibilities, to detect realities, and to situate different voices coming from different epistemic locations.

A Theology of the Crucified

Mary the mother of Jesus, as Luther presents her in his commentary on the Magnificat, is a good example of the first circumstance. She "looks not to the result of humility but with simple heart regards things of low degree, and gladly associates with them."[15] Luther writes:

> You must feel the pinch of poverty in the midst of your hunger and learn by experience what hunger and poverty are, with no provision on hand and no help in yourself or any other man, but in God only; so that the work may be God's alone and impossible to be done by any other. You must not only think and speak of a low estate but actually come to be in a low state and caught in it, without any human aid, so that God alone may do the work. Or if it should not go to pass, you must at least desire it and not shrink from it.[16]

In the cross, in suffering and humiliation, we can only utter the story of suffering from which God will deliver us, and with the same confidence cry out the lament of forsakenness. The theologian of the cross cannot speak *about* the cross from the standpoint of the cross itself; she can only speak from the cross in sheer faith without evidence, in complete trust amidst abandonment; in her radical refusal to say that evil is good. This location calls us to "simply be honest about the world"[17] and not to buffer the cries that come from crosses even today, not to stifle the "deafening cry" of the oppressed (as Medellín, the 1968 Latin American Episcopal Conference, called it) which still resounds today as it did then at Calvary: "My God, my God, why have you forsaken me." Faith and the "deafening cry" do not cancel each other.

---

[15] Martin Luther, "The Magnificat," *Luther's Works* vol. 21 *The Sermon on the Mount and the Magnificat*, ed. Jaroslav Pelikan, trans. A. T. W. Steinhaeuser (St. Louis: Concordia, 1956), 173–74.

[16] Ibid., 347–48.

[17] Jon Sobrino, *Jesus the Liberator* (Maryknoll, N.Y.: Orbis Books, 1993), 234.

Consider the short dialogue between Jesus and the criminal executed at his side (Luke 23:39-43). The scene narrated by the evangelist produces the mixture of styles typical of biblical literature, the extreme "pendulation" between *sublimitas* and *humilitas*, as Auerbach has argued.[18] There is such simplicity in the scene; it surprises us by turning the worst fate into unimaginable lustrous promise of glory. Jorge Luis Borges conveys this in a poem that might serve as the most pertinent commentary on a "theology of the crucified" ever produced:

Luke XXIII

Gentile or Jew or simply a man
Whose face has been lost in time,
We shall not have the silent
Letters of oblivion.

What could he know of forgiveness,
A thief whom Judea nailed to a cross?
For us those days are lost.
During his last undertaking,

Death by crucifixion,
He learned from the taunts of the crowd
That the man who was dying beside him
Was God. And blindly he said:

*Remember me when thou comest
Into thy kingdom*, and from the terrible cross
The unimaginable voice
Which one day will judge us all

---

[18] Erich Auerbach, *Mimesis: The Representation of Reality in Western Literature* (Princeton: Princeton University Press, 1953), 72, 151.

Promised him Paradise. Nothing more was said
Between them before the end came,
But history will not let the memory
Of their last afternoon die.

O friends, the innocence of this friend
Of Jesus! That simplicity which made him,
From the disgrace of punishment, ask for
And be granted Paradise

Was what drove him time
And again to sin and to bloody crime.[19]

Cross and paradise, shame and glory meet each other. The bluntness that led the robber time and again into sin and crime was that which made him ask and be granted paradise. Nothing else was required from him that he did not have before, even if it had been employed for sinful ends. As it reads so well in the original: "…ese candor que hizo que pediera y ganara el Paraíso…era el que tantas vezes al pecado lo arrojó y al azar ensangrentado."[20] The theologian of the cross, as the one hanging on the cross, does not pronounce a theology of the cross, in the objective sense of the genitive. From the cross comes only a plea: "remember me."

Theology at the Cross Deriding

The second location in relationship to the cross is exemplified by the second criminal who challenges Jesus' credentials, and by those at the foot of the cross who mockingly told the physician to heal himself. Be it sarcasm, as in the Gospel narratives, or a pious practice from medieval Christendom, or modern-day spiritual techniques that promise prosperity,

[19] Jorge Luis Borges, *Selected Poems*, ed. Alexander Coleman, trans. Mark Strand (New York: Viking, 1999), 131.
[20] Ibid., 130. The leitmotiv of friendship lifted up toward the end of the poem is the hermeneutical key used by Deanna A. Thompson in *Crossing the Divide: Luther, Feminism, and the Cross* (Minneapolis: Fortress Press, 2004).

the basic attitude seems the same: it is tempting God in Christ; it is placing Christ on trial.

This tempted Christ (*angefochtene Christus*) is invited to deliver signs of power and glory at his moment of trial. He knew who the tempter was from his desert experience and he knew that, "It is said, 'You shall not tempt the Lord your God'" (Luke 4:12). Here one of the basic characteristics of the theologian of glory is manifested in the precise reversal of the relationship between what God does and who God is. The theologian of glory speculates behind the visible in search for the invisible, and in doing so looks for something visible that would serve as an indication of the invisible.

Such theology prioritizes the work produced, both human and divine, above the knowledge of God. The theologian of glory is the one who says: "Show me what you do and I will believe who you are." The theologian of the cross says: "I know who you are for I have seen you there in the midst of brokenness."

The parable of the great judgment of Matthew 25 is a shocking narrative for those who pretend to know (or think they know) who Christ is (Christians!) by what Christ does and reveals in his glory. The parable is not a moral instruction to feed the poor, clothe the naked, visit the sick, and so forth. Rather, it is about a cognitively dissonant surprise. Those who attended the needs of the little ones did it without knowing that they were doing it to Christ himself. They did not recognize Christ in the faces of those they helped. The condemned pleaded their case saying that also they did not recognize Christ in the faces of those little ones, implying that they supposed they knew who Jesus was. In their "knowledge" of Christ, they missed Jesus, for they could see in the cross only a criminal who boasted that he was a king being executed. Instead of being poor, sick, jailed, and hungry, if only Christ had shown some of his glory, they would then, only then, have seen him. As Barth remarked, Christ is not only God in the flesh, but under the condition of utter sinfulness.

Theology Away from the Cross

The third location in relation to the cross is the one taken by most of the disciples who, according to the Gospel narratives, ran and hid from the cross. Here there is no theology of the cross. Those who ran saw the cross as a tragic event, a death that no longer belonged to the world, a tragic end with no intrinsic meaning except for pointing back to the life of Jesus. Their explanation and interpretation is that the true prophet dies, as we can find in the dominant motif accounting for Jesus' death in the speech of Stephen in Acts 7:52: "Which of the prophets did your ancestors not persecute? They killed those who foretold the coming of the Righteous One, and now you have become his betrayers and murderers." Most of the disciples stayed away from the cross, carrying with them the memories of the life of Jesus; the rest was left behind in a tomb.

Illustrative is the story of the two disciples who took off walking toward Emmaus, as recounted in Luke 24. On their way Jesus was certainly remembered as the one who walked over water (to use the image of Machado's poem), Jesus who was alive in the stories told about him before his death or even apart from his having gone through death. He resurrects, so to say, in the tales told about him. Here the cross does represent the closing of the meaning of one's life, but lies outside of and is, most importantly, not the fulfillment of life's meaning, only its consummation.

They are moving away from the cross as if to say, this is the way things are and it is over. They are joined by another who tells them the story leading to the cross as the prophets foretold it. They are given a frame within which the meaning could be attained. They needed the story to be brought back to the cross, but the story itself does not do it, because the story cannot contain the point or provide the "ah-ha" experience, the "Oh, now I see." The point of the cross does not end—it does not even start—at its portrayed meaning, whatever that might be. The point is to encounter the living God concealed in its opposite, as Luther would say (working with his apocalyptic reversals). And this they will only understand after the story is over and the body is once more symbolically broken.

This lifts another important implication of the theology of the cross. The theology of the cross is not an intratextual event. It is not the discourse, the explanation, or the interpretation that brings about the revelation of meaning, even if the hermeneutist is Jesus himself. It is an event that does not settle itself within the frame of meaning of the narrative. Though their hearts were "burning within" them while they were being instructed about the Scriptures, it was only after the hermeneutics ended that the revelation happened in the breaking of the bread. As the nineteenth-century Cuban writer and nationalist hero José Martí used to say, "Sometimes the best way to say something is to do it." The story is a propaedeutic, but its meaning lies beyond its own confine; or better said, what it reveals happens at the exact moment after the discourse ends, outside the text. Not even in the story of the cross is there a theology of the cross. It becomes a theology of the cross when the story ends, and the present broken body is presented and beheld. The theologian that runs from the cross has the story of Jesus but is unable to read it in the light and darkness of the cross itself. It is only the darkness of the approaching night (v. 29) that reveals the "light" with the breaking of the bread. Then the disciples return immediately to Jerusalem, to the place they left behind, the place of the crucifixion, even as they had retired for the night to rest. The story is about a conversion, a turning around and engaging a new practice.

Theology of the Cross as a Practice of Resurrection

Theology of the cross as a dispositional practice (*usus*) is a theology that stands in the face of the cross but responds to it with the confidence that the cross is not outside of God's providence, promising or terrible as it might be. An example is again found in Luther's 1521 commentary on the Magnificat: the description of Mary, the lowly maid who recognizes without yet having evidence that God raises her and all those of low degree, because she saw her own self as meriting nothing but God's own infinite empowerment and grace while still under disgrace. But more important, it was she who, with other women, is reported to have been at the foot of the cross. Even if no Magnificat was sung there, Mary's actions were a testimony to what could be called a practice of resurrection. For those women that cross was not yet the end of it all; there was still a labor to be done.

As the lowly womb of a poor peasant girl from an insignificant Galilean village could bear God (*theotokos*), so also the tomb in which the body of Jesus was laid should be honored with the best they could offer. The one who died that shameful death was not finished for them. Luke tells us that the women who were at the foot of the cross went to see where his body was laid. And after they had seen the dead body of Jesus put into the tomb, they went home to prepare the ointments and spices for the broken body. After the preparation and observing the Shabbat, they returned to the tomb to anoint a putrescent dead body only to be surprised and terrified to find the tomb empty and that very same body alive. (We, too, are scared when we encounter genuine newness, as those women were, in face of experiences of redemption and resurrection; it is always easier to manage grief than the unexpected, for that lies outside of our control.) The surprise is there when they carry out a labor of mourning and love. In the midst of their pain, in the face of the slain body of the Beloved One, those women practiced the unlikely act of love without expecting it ever to be returned. A theology of the cross is always the other side of a practice of resurrection, and a resurrection practice is the other side of a theology of the cross.

Wendell Berry put this practice of resurrection remarkably well in a poem entitled "The Way of Pain."

> I read of Christ crucified
> the only begotten son
> sacrificed to flesh and time
> and all our woe. He died
> and rose, but who does not tremble
> for his pain, his loneliness,
> and the darkness of the sixth hour?
> Unless we grieve like Mary
> at His grave, giving Him up
> as lost, no Easter morning comes.[21]

---

[21] Wendell Berry, *Collected Poems* (San Francisco: North Point, 1985), 210.

It is this practice that connects the resurrection to the cross and pre-figures the community of those who in proclamation and communion hope against all hope. This is the practice that keeps history open, open to revisit even its past of victimization and suffering. This is the task of the followers of Christ: not to allow history to end in calamity, not to allow the past to be closed, against all evidence, against all hope.

In 1937 the Jewish German philosopher Walter Benjamin wrote the following in an article published in a journal edited by his friend and colleague Max Horkheimer: "The work of the past is not closed for the historical materialist. He cannot see the work of an epoch, or any part of it, as reified, as literally placed on one's lap."[22] A sharp criticism ensues from Horkheimer in which he writes to Benjamin: "The supposi-tion of the unclosed past is idealistic.... Past injustice has occurred and [history] is closed. Those who were slain in it were truly slain....In the end, your statements are theological."[23] Benjamin retorts, establishing a discussion that is one of the most significant theological debates of the twentieth century, perhaps because it took place outside the faculties of theology:

> The corrective for this sort of thinking lies in the reflection that history is not simply a science but a form of empathetic memory [*Eingedenken*]. What science has "settled," empathetic memory can modify. It can transform the unclosed (happiness) into something closed and the closed (suffering) into something unclosed. That is theology, certainly, but in empathetic memory we have an experience that prohibits us from conceiving history completely non-theologically.[24]

This empathetic memory is capable of opening the closed past. Hork-heimer played the role of the disciples on the way to Emmaus. He left the tragedy closed and behind; Calvary was no longer redeemable. Benjamin,

---

[22] Walter Benjamin, *Ausgewählte Schriften II* (Frankfurt: Suhrkamp, 1955), 311.
[23] Cited by Helmut Peukert, *Science, Action, and Fundamental Theology: Toward a Theology of Com-municative Action* (Cambridge: MIT Press, 1984), 206–07.
[24] Ibid., 207.

like the women in the Gospels, kept the empathetic memory, against all evidences, against all science, in a practice of resurrection that carried them to the Easter Sunday.

The connection of the resurrection to the cross is a pilgrimage to the tomb. The surprise comes when a labor of love and mourning is carried through. Only after one prepares the spices for a body that will not be able to utter even a word of thanks, only then might a surprise come about. But there is no guarantee issued in advance. As Wendell Berry said: "Unless we grieve like Mary at His grave, giving Him up as lost, no Easter morning comes." Such a grief, such a labor of love and mourning grows out of the faith and hope that no gesture of love will ever be lost even if nothing can be changed, even if the wrong must be accepted for the sake of love. Danish theologian Anna Marie Aagaard speaks, in this regard, of a theology of tears in a lecture entitled "Cry of Agony and Bread of Tears":

> The moaning over the wrong that is accepted is visible in the faces of human beings, even when the tears have gone. It leaves its traces. It is holy; it belongs to God, for no human being can share it. No-one but I can, by myself, decide to preserve the love to the one or those who trample on my life so that I for the sake of love accept to be wretched— and that without hope of change in the state of things. For, should they be changed, I would have to betray love, and that is the sin that cannot be forgiven. There is nothing else to do but to love—and to weep! This is to save the world for the sake of love. It happens around us—with immense costs. Theologically, we call this "to save", and faith senses God's presence therein.[25]

There is a short story by Gabriel García Marquez that conveys well this idea of a labor of mourning and love I am trying to express. The story, published in 1968, is called "The Handsomest Drowned Man in the World." The author wrote this only some years after the first of the

---

[25] Cited by Else Marie Wiberg Pedersen, "'The Holy Spirit shall come upon you:' Mary—the Human 'Locus' for the Holy Spirit," in *Cracks in the Walls: Essays on Spirituality, Ecumenicity and Ethics*, ed. Else Marie Wiberg Pedersen and Johannes Nissen (Frankfurt a/M: Peter Lang, 2005), 24.

military coups took place that would spread all over Latin America (Brazil 1964, Argentina 1965, and Chile 1971) with their practice of dumping enemies of the régime on the high seas. Many would eventually be washed ashore (before Chile improved the "technology" by placing a large piece of metal in the bowels of the victims before throwing them into the ocean). Gárcia Marquez might have had this in mind when he wrote the story, which makes it really a story about reclaiming a past, of unclosing it by an empathetic memory.

According to Gárcia Marquez's story, in a small village of fishermen off the Colombian coast of the Caribbean Sea a drowned man is washed to shore. He is found by the villagers and brought into town. While the women start preparing his body for a proper funeral the men go around nearby villages to see if someone is missing. They come back with the news that he was not a habitant of the region. The women were already imagining places and experiences he has been through, filling that corpse with a fantastic life, giving him a name, Esteban, and assigning him parents and relatives so that the whole village was, through him, related to each other. When the news came that he did not belong to any of the villages nearby, there was jubilation in the midst of tears: "'Praise God,' they sighed, 'he's ours!'" After preparing the body of the drowned man who "was the tallest, strongest, most virile, and best built man they have ever seen," they return him to the ocean dressed in new clothes they had to tailor, for his size was larger than any one they knew. Fully adorned with flowers, the body is carried in procession to the cleft on the rocks by the ocean where their dead ones were released to the waters. And so the story ends:

> While they fought for the privilege of carrying him on their shoulders…men and women became aware for the first time of the desolation of their streets, the dryness of the courtyards, the narrowness of their dreams as they faced the splendor and beauty of their drowned man. They let him go without anchor so that he could come back if he wished and whenever he wished, and they all held their breath for the fraction of centuries the body took to fall into the abyss. They did not need to look at one another to realize that they were not whole, and they would never be. But they also knew that everything would be different from

then on, that their houses would have wider doors, higher ceilings, and stronger floors so that Esteban's memory could go everywhere without bumping into beams,…they were going to paint their house fronts with gay colors to make Esteban's memory eternal and they were going to break their back digging for springs among the stones and planting flowers on the cliffs so that in future years at dawn the passengers on great liners would awaken, suffocated with the smell of gardens on the high sea, and the captain would have to come down from the bridge in his dress uniform…pointing to the promontory of roses on the horizon, he would say in fourteen languages, look there, where the wind is so peaceful now that it's gone to sleep beneath the beds, over there, where the sun's so bright that the sunflowers don't know which way to turn, yes, over there, that's Esteban's village.[26]

Returning to the Gospel narrative, one sees that in the midst of pain and desolation, in the face of the slain body of the beloved one, those women practiced the unlikely act of love not expecting any return. This is a labor of love and mourning. In the words of Kierkegaard,

If one wants to make sure that love is completely unselfish, he eliminates every possibility of repayment. But precisely this is eliminated in the relationship to one who is dead. If love nevertheless remains, it is in truth unselfish…. *The work of love in remembering one who is dead is a work of the* MOST UNSELFISH *love.*"[27]

A theology of the cross (*in usus passionis*) is always the other side of a practice of resurrection, and the other way around: a practice of resurrection can only be exercised in the face of the dismal experience of the cross that in the Shabbat is remembered and thus brought back.

---

[26] Gabriel García Márquez, "The Handsomest Drowned Man in the World," in *Collected Stories* (New York: Harper Collins, 1984), 253–54.

[27] Søren Kierkegaard, *Works of Love* (New York: Harper & Row, 1962), 320.

A "Theory" of the Cross

The Human Arts: *Poiesis, Praxis,* and *Theoria*

On the sabbath they rested according to the commandment.

Luke 23:56b

Is it preposterous to suggest that there is a theory of the cross? I suggest that it is not, in fact, preposterous—insofar as the word *theory* is not associated with, say, something bookish. In fact, it might be precisely the opposite, that which does not have an object and cannot become an object, like a book. It is more like an attitude one takes in face of events and things. How is it, then, that theology is associated with a systematic organization of propositions and thus lined up with the notion of theory? Let us consider the ways theology has been defined and how "theory" might be conceived.

"Faith in search of understanding" (*fides quaerens intellectum*) is Anselm's most concise and broadly accepted definition of theology. The Latin verb *quaero*, "to seek, to search for, to want, to desire" is normally used as a transitive verb; it applies to an object that is being sought or desired, in this case understanding. Considering the Protestant concept "by faith alone" (*sola fide*), however, it is proper to think about reading this Latin verb *quaero* that has faith as its subject in keeping Anselm's formula, as an *intransitive* verb without an object: "theology is faith seeking" or "theology is faith desiring."

To meet God in the cross is not rationally "intelligible." It is neither wisdom nor an evident sign, as Paul insists in the first chapter of 1 Corinthians. A theology of the cross is not about an object that faith seeks but about the very desiring of faith. Its longing can be for many things or for nothing at all; even for silence, absence, emptiness. Such a definition is certainly not exclusive. Theology can be and has been the examination of "faith desiring" that entails, first, an external object (promise and *hope*); can entail, second, pure relationality as its "object" (which is *love*); but, in the third place, might also be the intransitive desiring in solitude (which is desiring nothing but *faith itself*).

These three definitions are legitimate and complementary. Where the cross is concerned, the first leads to what has been called objective doctrines of atonement, (described earlier in connection with the apoteletic key). The second definition leads to subjective views of what the cross, by its exemplary character, teaches us about life and love. It is the third definition we are pursuing (even "pursuing" is misleading, as we shall see).

The relationship of faith to the objects it seeks is an old issue in theological discussions; we came to call it a question of the relationship between theory and practice. Theory is to seek understanding; practice is to accomplish something. Discussion is often confined to this choice: Is it a theory or a practice? Which should the theologian strive for? In Christian theology this concern was raised by the Alexandrian theologians Clement and Origen and later by Augustine in their interpretation of the Martha and Mary story. Mary is the one whose portion "will not be taken away" and Martha, one who is too concerned about nonessential, practical things (Luke 10:38-42). Martha and Mary became stereotypes for practice and theory. But what is this theory that Mary stands for? How is it related to the cross? Before we examine that, some background about the theory-versus-practice debate in the West.

We begin with Aristotle, a thinker Luther felt had little to offer to theology. At the beginning of Book VI of his *Metaphysics* the philosopher presents the three fundamental human arts or faculties: he calls them *theoria*, *praxis*, and *poiesis*.[1] While all three are forms of knowledge, each has a distinct intellectual structure (*episteme*) and function (*dianoia*).

---

[1] Aristotle, *Metaphysics*, Book VI.I.5 (E, 1025-28 b).

Theoria is defined by the observer's absorbing passivity or pure receptivity, which in medieval rules of spirituality was called *contemplatio*.[2] *Praxis* means doing something for the sake of doing it well, without an objective result sought or produced; its structure is determined by inter-subjective activity or performance. *Poiesis*, the root of the modern word *poetry*, aims at an objective lasting result or product.

The Greek theater serves as a good analogy for Aristotle's distinction of human arts. One who writes a play or builds the stage is engaged in *poiesis*, their activities result in production, a result of labor left objectively inscribed in the play, or erected in the stage and the setting. *Praxis* is what the performers do on stage; their acting does not result in an objective product; the end, the telos, of *praxis* is performing for the sake of doing it well. *Theoria* is the undisturbed attitude of the audience to capture attentively what is taking place on the stage. Although all three can sometimes take place simultaneously or overlap,[3] their discreet characteristics can be established.

This tripartite division of human arts has been largely supplanted in the Latin West by the customary binary way of dividing human arts between theory and action (*actio*) or else, since John Duns Scotus, between theory and *praxis* (which is not distinguished from *poiesis* but includes it). Theology has been alternately aligned with one or the other. Theology as "faith desiring" would develop in either direction, often seen as exclusive alternatives. It would be used to seek enlightenment or to seek and engage moral or practical endeavors, living a committed life and thus serving God and the world.

The distinction originally rooted in the polarity between *theologia* and *oeconomia* received different binary constructions through the history of Christian thought. In the early Middle Ages they were called *credenda* (that which is to be believed) and *agenda* (that which is to be acted upon);

---

[2] This was exactly the one rule Luther, in his revisiting of these rules of theology (*lectio, oratio,* and *contemplatio*), changed to *tentatio*, being upon a trial, which for Luther expressed the passive character he intended to convey, namely, a disposed passion, as opposed to contemplative's passivity.

[3] E.g., an actor might be improvising, thus producing a "text" that was not there before (which would be *poiesis*), but doing it while performing on stage (which would be *praxis*). The actor in case might be for a moment passively absorbed by what is taking place on stage (which would be *theoria*).

then came the opposing schools of Thomistic theory and Franciscan action, Orthodoxy and Pietism in the post-Reformation period, dogmatics and ethics since the seventeenth century, pure reason and practical reason since the Enlightenment, and with the emergence of liberation theology, orthodoxy, and orthopraxis. In theological education this distinction is disciplinarily inscribed in the division between theology and ministry. The classification is still alive in the ecumenical movement: two organizations that were joined to form the World Council of Churches are "Faith and Order" and "Life and Work." Although housed under one roof, the different units still bear conflicting strategies and objectives. More recently we find transcendental and contextual approaches to theology or distinguish between foundational and nonfoundational theologies. These dichotomies inhabit the Western binary tradition; binarism makes one concept always seem to be in opposition to the other…two terms always flank an axis on which one is nobler, superior, of more value than the other.

Poiesis and *Praxis*

This binary arrangement of the relationship between theory and practice is in part the result of the failure to distinguish between *poiesis* and *praxis* as discrete human arts. It has created confusion in the necessary theological distinctions between hope and love, promise and consolation, creation and atonement, the person and the work of Christ. In biblical exegesis this failure to differentiate has obscured the fine but precise distinction between the "poetic" and the narrative genres in the Scriptures, that is, between invocative or performative utterances on one hand and communicative discourse on the other. In the Gospels we have both, the words of Jesus that, when uttered, produced an objective result such as miracles or forgiveness of sins (called *poietic* acts), and Jesus' communicative utterances conveyed through parables and sermons that, while edifying, did not produce an objective result (conveyed by the notion of *praxis*).[4]

[4] The distinction is the one established in recent linguistic philosophy by J. L. Austin between illocutionary and perlocutionary acts. Illocutionary acts are utterances that do what they are saying, while perlocution describe acts that simply state affairs as in the midst of a conversation. See J. L. Austin, *How to Do Things with Words* (Cambridge: Harvard University Press, 1962), 108–09.

The distinction between *poiesis* and *praxis* returned to theology with the emergence of liberation and political theologies in the late 1960s, bringing into crisis (in its etymological sense of "scission") the binary scheme that sets "theory" and "praxis" as the polarities that blur the distinction between *poiesis* and *praxis*.[5] A distinction between two forms of "practice" began to be recognized, while the call to seek understanding was being used for the very purpose of bringing about this distinction. What was called theory was employed to establish the distinction between *poiesis* and *praxis* and their epistemic claims.

In Europe and to a certain extent in the United States, political theology was working with a concept of praxis that resembled the original connotation of the word, that of exercising the interactive, discerning, and communicative life of the polis. In its turn liberation theology, as originally developed in Latin America and by black theology in the United States, stressed a concept of praxis closer to the Greek *poiesis*. The creative or productive dimension of practice was emphasized to the point of understanding labor not only as production but also to include human self-production, as it appears for the first time in modern times in G. W. F. Hegel and more explicitly in Karl Marx. Political theology was inspired by the Frankfurt School of Social Research, particularly the work of Jürgen Habermas and his definition of praxis as "communicative action." Latin American liberation theology, inspired by thinkers like Paulo Freire, stressed the productive dimension of praxis, the creation of a new society. This distinction is not a separation. As the two theologies developed, they certainly learned from each other, but were aware of their differences.

Complementarity

In the mid 1970s Jürgen Moltmann wrote an "Open Letter to José Míguez-Bonino,"[6] criticizing five Latin American theologians, including

---

[5] The discrete characteristics of *praxis* and *poiesis* can be recognized as standing behind the distinction between sacrament and word, respectively. The consequences of this parallelism are very suggestive, but cannot be expanded upon in this context.

[6] Jürgen Moltmann, "An Open Letter to José Míguez-Bonino," *Christianity and Crisis* (March 29, 1976), 57–63.

Míguez-Bonino. He noted the use of Marx's understanding of labor (in the sense of *poiesis*) and raised questions on it from a more *praxis*-oriented stance as communicative action. In a response article Hugo Assmann said that creative production was the one fundamental right of human beings; proper and just political practice would follow.[7]

Obviously, context counts. European political theology worked out of affluent societies in which distributive justice was the fundamental issue and the delusions of a new society (proclaimed in the eastern European countries under socialist régimes) was becoming obvious. Liberation theology emerged from a continent that was largely under military régimes. They suppressed virtually all the mechanisms of civil society that could allow for a political way out. A new society had to be built before a new political practice could be exercised. The distinction (probably originating with Freire) was between "freedom from" and "freedom for," or between the North Atlantic stress on a negative definition of freedom and the southern emphasis on an attributive notion of justice (and a constructive notion of freedom).

The fact that this distinction in the Western concept of *praxis* reintroduces the classical Greek distinction between *praxis* and *poiesis* is really nothing new. Hegel introduced it in Western modernity in the "Master and the Slave Dialectics" chapter of his *Phenomenology*,[8] a text that clearly distinguishes the interaction (Greek: *praxis*) between slave and master, and the slave's labor (Greek: *poiesis*).[9] This distinction was even more sharply

---

[7] Hugo Assmann, "Breves consideraciones al margen del informe final del encuentro de Oaxtepec," *Estudios Ecuménicos* 38 (1979): 50–52. See also Vítor Westhelle, "Labor: A Suggestion for Rethinking the Way of the Christian," *Word & World* 4, no. 2 (1986): 194–206. Shortly after this initial exchange, a condemnation of Latin American liberation theology was issued by German Roman Catholic bishops. In turn, Moltmann, along with other theologians, signed a letter of protest in defense of liberation theology. Letters of response to Moltmann's original "Open Letter" by the theologians criticized were written, but due to Moltmann's gesture of support were never published. This established not only the awareness of the different notions of "praxis" with which they were working, but also established a conversation about their complementarities.

[8] Hegel, *Werke* (Frankfurt a/M: Suhrkamp, 1970) 3:145–55.

[9] It is therefore not a coincidence that this chapter of the *Phenomenology* plays a crucial role in Freire's influential notion of *conscientização*, the termination being the same as in *ação* (action), but the examples he uses makes it rather rhyme with *produção* (production), and it is, therefore, poorly rendered in English as "consciousness raising."

developed in the growing awareness of the young Marx's privileging the concept of political *praxis*, while the older Marx insisted on the primacy of productive labor (*poiesis*) and abandoned *praxis* as a foundational category. The dispute is: What conditions what? Do politics determine economy or is it the reverse?

Following this development of the idea of praxis we will see that the common notion of theory, associated with the working of the intellect, is part of both communicative action and productive labor; both engage intellectual operations. This brings us back to the original Aristotelian definitions of *praxis* and *poiesis* as forms of "knowledge" (or intellection) involving an action and the use of mental faculties (*dianoia*). Understanding mental operations as actions has been prevalent in the West since William of Ockham argued that mental processes in themselves are practices. It was only with Antonio Gramsci, in the beginning of the twentieth century, that the notion of intellectual labor (*lavoro intellettuale*) would connect the notion of intellection with interactive communication and also with the production of knowledge as an objective reality, which should properly be labeled "poetry."[10]

Distinction and emphasis must not imply separation. *Praxis* or *poiesis* become distorted when isolated from each other. *Poiesis* without *praxis* is blind and enslaving—lacks solidarity, love; *praxis* without *poiesis* is empty activism—lacks novelty, promise, and hope.

An illustration might convey my point here. Swedish film director Ingmar Bergman, when asked about the intention and purpose of his films, responded with a tale that makes clear the distinction between *poiesis* and *praxis*. Bergman said:

> There is an old story of how the cathedral of Chartres was struck by lightning and burned to the ground. Then thousands of people came from all points of the compass, like a giant procession of ants, and together they began to rebuild the cathedral on its old site. They worked until the building was completed—master builders, artists, labourers,

---

[10] The influence of Gramsci's ideas in the beginning of liberation theology is by now well established. See Ofelia Schutte, *Cultural Identity and Social Liberation in Latin American Thought* (Albany: State University of New York Press, 1993), 169.

clowns, noblemen, priests, burghers. But they all remained anonymous, and no one knows to this day who built the cathedral of Chartres. Regardless of my own beliefs and doubts, which are unimportant in this connection, it is my opinion that art lost its basic creative drive the moment it was separated from worship. It severed an umbilical cord and now lives its own sterile life, generating and degenerating itself. In former days the artist's…work was to the glory of God….Today the individual has become the highest form and the greatest bane of artistic creation….The individualists stare at each other's eyes and deny the existence of each other.[11]

Bergman's story points to the symbiosis between *poiesis* and *praxis*, while recognizing the distinction between the collaborative equality and interaction of those who gathered together from all classes, trades, and places, and the creative, constructive work of building a cathedral that is a classic example of high gothic architecture.

If the acknowledgment of the distinction between *praxis* and *poiesis* brought the recognition that each, in different ways, implied intellection, what then is *theoria*? This is what we need to examine. The occasion is already presented by Bergman's story. Those engaged in *poiesis* and *praxis* were doing it for the building of a cathedral, a place of worship, which brings us, finally, to this remaining human faculty in Aristotle's classification: *theoria*.

Theoria

To approach *theoria* a break is needed, a rupture with the quotidian, with everyday life, even with this very discourse in which we are engaged. *Theoria* technically means contemplation, observance, gazing, speculation, looking at, beholding, which also implies, therefore, leisure, passive receptivity. Quite different from the "bookish" connotations it often has received, it is rather close to what in the Jewish-Christian tradition is celebrated as the Shabbat, the day to break with the quotidian, with everyday life and

---

[11] Ingmar Bergman, *The Seventh Seal* (New York: Simon & Schuster, 1960), 8–9.

its chores, to abstain from work in order to behold. For Walter Benjamin, describing the Shabbat, it is the "initial day of the calendar [that] serves as historical time-lapse camera. And, basically it is the same day that keeps recurring in the guise of holidays, which are days of remembrance."[12] The Shabbat is about observance, remembrance: *theoria*!

The difference between the Aristotelian view of *theoria* and the Jewish-Christian Shabbat should not be overlooked, however. The Jewish-Christian Shabbat departs from the Aristotelian *theoria*, as the contemplation of the supreme good, beauty, and truth, by establishing an unbridgeable abyss between God, the poet, and our poetic endeavors; between God, the communicant, and we as communicators. In spite of this abyss an analogical argument is allowed between divine *poiesis* and *praxis*, creation and incarnation, on the one hand, and our labor and actions on the other. Nevertheless, unique in the Jewish-Christian transcendent and unbridgeable gap between God and creation is the establishment of an ironic rupture between the two, a disruption in the smoothness of the analogy, a Kierkegaardian-like discontinuity that cannot be uttered. Yet it remains there as an unquenchable apophatic silence. In the Shabbat, God "observes" the divine work accomplished, but we are called to observe not ours, but God's.

This radical difference of perspectives needs to be recognized in its awesome dimensions. While the Aristotelian *theoria* was full of confidence and fascination with the process of reception and its processing by the human intellect, the Jewish-Christian Shabbat, though certainly sharing also confidence, demands prostration in face of the unutterable *tremendum*. *Tremendum*: the quaking awareness of an awesome otherness. In the words of Cyril of Alexandria: *siope proskyneistho to arreton*, "in silence I fall on my knees to worship the unspeakable."[13]

In the biblical narrative there are two passages laid out almost symmetrically, connecting the Hebrew Bible and the New Testament under the same motif of *theoria*. The first comes at the beginning of the Hebrew text, the other at the end of the Gospels. What they have in common is that both have to do with the Shabbat, the Jewish-Christian version

---

[12] Walter Benjamin, *Illuminations* (New York: Schocken, 1968), 261.
[13] Cited by Dietrich Bonhoeffer, *Wer ist und wer war Jesus Christus* (Hamburg: Furche, 1962), 9.

of *theoria*. The first points to the *fascinans*, that which enthralls, charms, and absorbs, the other to the *tremendum* that which makes us quake and tremble.

Fascinans

The first passage is the account of the creation story that reaches its apex with the institution of the day of rest, after six days of God's labor culminating in the creation of human beings. In the Septuagint the verb used for God's creative activity is the very Greek *poieo*, to work productively (which is, incidentally, the same verb that normally describes Jesus' miracles, the novelty of water turned into wine, the lame walking, or the dead rising). We still keep this notion in the Greek wording of the Nicene Creed when we confess God to be literally the "poet of heaven and earth" (*poieten ouranou kai ges*). The Shabbat culminates the narrative by announcing that the first day of human beings was the day of rest, the day of breaking with the quotidian; human beings begin as theoreticians, leisurely contemplating on their first day of existence the work that has been done and venerating their creator. Human communicative interaction, *praxis*, would follow later in the narrative and culminates in the assassination of Abel.[14] The Shabbat emerges, however, as an institution or an order of creation, as it used to be called; it is the earthly frame of what Christians would later call *ekklesia*, the rupture with the toils of everyday for the sake of *theoria*. To use the basic medieval categories in order to describe the fundamental institutions of creation, we could line them up fairly well with *oikonomia*, *ecclesia*, and *politia*, which engage the basic human faculties of *poiesis*, *theoria*, and *praxis*, respectively. First comes creation, then comes the Shabbat, and human interaction follows.

---

[14] Actually, the first time that a communicative interaction among humans is explicitly registered in the biblical narrative, the first time a human being explicitly addresses another is when Cain said to Abel: "Let us go out to the field." See Vítor Westhelle, "'The Noble Tribe of Truth': Etchings on Myth, Language, and Truth Speaking," in *Grundtvig in International Perspectice: Studies in the Creativity of Interaction*, ed. A. M. Allchin, S. A. J. Bradley, N. A. Hjelm, and J. H. Schørring (Aarhus: Aarhus University Press, 2000), 87–102.

Tremendum

Yet not all is delightfully marvelous and charmingly fascinating. The other narrative is found at the end of the canonical Gospels, in which the last days and hours of Jesus' activities are narrated, culminating in his execution and his resurrection on the day following the Shabbat. Often overlooked in our liturgies and theologies, this Shabbat, this particular day of observance inserted between Good Friday and Easter Sunday, is quite significant in the way it mirrors that first Shabbat of Genesis. Just after what Paul called the "apocalypse of Jesus Christ" (Gal. 1:12) took place, we have this intriguing account of the women who were eyewitnesses to Jesus' crucifixion and burial. After having followed that gruesome tragedy, they presumably go out to the market in order to get some herbs and oil to prepare some balm to anoint the defunct body of the Beloved One.[15]

Yet, then, at that point, the narrative suddenly halts and it simply says that the Shabbat arrived and they observed it, according to the commandment. Even what they might have been "doing," like prayers, mediation, sobbing in remembrance of the events just past, is not registered. The narrative itself does what it announces: it halts in face of the unspeakable; it is the Shabbat, pure Jewish-Christian theory.

The narrative then resumes, after the Shabbat is over, when the women go out early in the morning to the tomb with what they had prepared, only to find that tomb empty and new life being announced, a new creation. What we find in the structure of this narrative is the mirror image of the narrative structure of the first chapters in Genesis. As it is implausible that the human beings would start the first day of their existence in pure contemplation, leisure, and adoration, it is also implausible to think that those women, in the middle of what for them was nothing less than an apocalypse with its most terrifying connotations, go and rest in observance of a commandment of a God who was apparently negligent in face of the terrible tragedy just witnessed. What we have in this latter narrative

---

[15] Mark 16:1 has them buying the spices and preparing them after the Shabbat, while Luke 23:56 places these actions before the Shabbat.

sequence reverses, as in a mirror image, the ordering of the same categories used above to frame the Genesis account. While in Genesis *poiesis* (creation) is followed by *theoria* (Shabbat) and then by *praxis* (human interaction), here the *praxis* of Jesus (his interaction) leads to his death. An unlikely moment of contemplation, rest, *theoria*, comes next (at least for those women in the evangelical narrative). This is followed by a new creation, a *poiesis*, which closes the cycle with the resurrection account, but only after the Shabbat of utter emptiness is over. And it needs to be first endured and mourned.

The implications of such an understanding of the human arts or faculties are significant for a theology of the cross in a number of ways, the least of which is not that it overcomes many of the problems inherited by the opposition between theory and practice, intellect and action. It implies that any form of action—creative or performative, productive or communicative—demands intellectual labor, or what has often been called "theory." And in every intellectual work there is always a knowledge that implies either a performative and communicative action or a creative production, if not both. However, the Jewish-Christian Shabbat as *theoria* is in fact the suspension of both, of *praxis* and *poiesis*—and of their intellectual operations as well! It is the moment in which one is receptive, passive, idle, playful, not intervening, not negotiating (*negotium* is a negative concept, it means *nec-otium*, the absence of leisure), at ease (which comes for *ad-iacere* "adjacency," lying by), and finally death itself as the absolute fulfillment of *theoria*. In other words, the Shabbat is a little death undertaken as a sacrifice.

In a letter Luther sent from Coburg, where he was staying during the Diet of Augsburg, to Melanchthon, who was in Augsburg to defend the confession of the Reformation in 1530, he counsels his fellow reformer: "Indeed to God leisure is a service; yes, there is nothing greater than leisure. For that very reason He wanted the Shabbat to be so rigidly observed."[16]

---

[16] *Deo eitiam servitor otio, imo nulla re magis quam otio. Ideo enim sabbathum voluit tam rigide prae caeteris servari. WA Br 5, 317, 40f (Nr 1516).*

Apousia

The close association between leisure, a "do-nothing" (*otium*) and death should not be surprising. In Christian symbolism it is represented by baptism as a dying—not a cleansing!—for the entering into a newness of life that grounds the community. We normally associate the Shabbat or the Christian worship with presence, as the time to encounter God. But it is only so, if so at all, because it is first of all the moment of absence. British writer Monica Furlong made an interesting observation, pertinent to the experience of Shabbat and particularly relevant for the Shabbat between Good Friday and Easter.

> It is costumary to talk as if the purpose of the Church has been to put people in touch with God, or to keep them in touch with God....although in face of it [the church] seems to exist to help its adherents into relationship with God, it equally, and perhaps essentially, plays the opposite role of trying to filter out an experience of transcendence which might be overwhelming.[17]

The church in this sense is engaged in *poiesis* (the sacramental acts) and in *praxis* (the sharing of the Word). But *theoria* is what happens in the interstices before, after, and in the midst of all that is devised to "protect" us from the experience of utter otherness, which is often the experience of awe in face of emptiness and the deep void. Both, in the Genesis account and in the Shabbat before Easter in the Gospels' account, the experience is of a God who is absent, not active, not creative, not even interactive. This is itself the moment of desiring in its most simple and intransitive form, this longing in the midst of the experience of utter emptiness, of absence, *apousia*, the moment in which desire cannot name its own object because it is simply the ineffable void itself. Here there is no *parousia*, no presence, no coming. The coming presence of the Messiah will be something else, it will last from Shabbat to Shabbat (Isa. 66:23), and there will be no longer

---

[17] Monica Furlong, *Contemplating Now* (Cambridge, Mass.: Cowley, 1983), 36.

days of toil, reason why there will be no need for a day of rest, no need for *theoria*. The New Jerusalem has no sanctuary (Rev. 21:22). Faith desiring is, however, the faith that longs for the object of its desire, while there is none. This is what theology is also about: to understand this desiring that makes itself manifest in the utter absence of what it longs for, but it does not name it, and it does not know it in any objective sense.

In 1690 or 1691, Sor Juana Inés de la Cruz, arguably the greatest theologian that the colonial Americas has produced, wrote a long essay entitled "Carta Atenegórica" ("Letter in an Athenian Style"), in which she takes issue with a sermon from the one who was considered the greatest preacher of the time, the Jesuit António Vieira.[18] The "Letter" is in itself the occasion for the most tragic turn in the life of Sor Juana, which makes some forget what the content of the text was. It is a daring and surprising argument written in the high baroque style that the author mastered as few ever have. The argument is about the greatest kindness that Christ has shown us (*las finezas de Cristo*[19]). After discussing the opinions of Augustine, Thomas Aquinas, and Chrysostom, in this order, she goes for what she calls the "Achilles' heel" in Vieira's argument. The famous Jesuit preacher, diplomat, and missionary had made the argument that the greatest kindness Jesus had shown was to love without reciprocity, which the washing of the feet of his disciples would illustrate. In a fascinating and dialectical way, Sor Juana argues that although this is a gesture of kindness, the greatest gesture of kindness of Christ was to absent himself so that we would not make bad use of what we receive, but would be allowed to act out of what we have already received. And she concludes with the admonition "that to ponder about his benefits [should] not remain speculative discourses, but that it turns into practical services, so that his negative benefits become in us positive ones finding in ourselves proper disposition."[20]

---

[18] Sor Juana Inés de la Cruz, *Obras Completas* (Mexico: Porrúa, 1981), 811–27.

[19] The Spanish *fineza* was common in baroque amorous writings, and appears frequently in Sor Juana's poetry. Her use of it here suggests that the debate with Vieira, about *las finezas de Cristo* is about a particular understanding of what grace means.

[20] Inés de la Cruz, *Obras*, 827.

For Sor Juana the "absence" of God implied a messianic presence that happens not in what she called "speculative discourses" but in practice. The genius of her argument is that the "theoretical" passivity and receptivity of what is sheer emptiness and absence (the "negative benefit of Christ") is that which brings life, a hidden indwelling presence. While most of the tradition of modern liberal theology insists on the *pro nobis* of God's relationship to the world, and while the recent neoorthodox tradition has insisted in the *extra nos* of God, Sor Juana reminds us of the words of Jesus in the Gospel of John: "It is to your advantage that I go away, for if I do not go away, the Advocate will not come to you" (John 16:7). Sor Juana, in a crisp and paradoxical way, reminds us of the third classical mode of God's relation to us: *in nobis*. And it is so precisely and paradoxically because the experience is that of absence. In her novel *The Color Purple* Alice Walker includes these words in a letter written by her character Celie:

> She say, Celie, tell the truth, have you ever found God in church? I never did. I just found a bunch of folks hoping for him to show. Any God I ever felt in church I brought with me. And I think all the other folks did too. They come to church to *share* God, not to find God.[21]

Walker's character complements the commentary by Furlong, the Shabbat of pure naked faith is broached by the church as much as it is also deflected by its rites and practices.

Care

To return to the Gospel narrative about the women keeping the Shabbat even after the Passion of the Beloved, it was out of that experience of immense void and because of it they went to the tomb early morning the next day, to find their own emptiness replaced by the emptiness of the tomb in which they expected to find presence—a dead presence, yet

---

[21] Alice Walker, *The Color Purple* (New York: Pocket Books, 1982), 200–01.

a presence. Instead, there was the absence of an absence. In that labor of mourning and love, the absence observed in that horrific Shabbat was redoubled in the absence of a corpse in that tomb—not even a corpse was there to fill the emptiness. In that absence of absences the messianic presence was uttered: "Go to meet him in Galilee." The *poietic* moment of the resurrection leads to a new encounter, a *praxis*. Not often realized in the commentaries on these sequence of events, however, is the "role" that the Shabbat plays in it, almost suggesting that there would not be a resurrection of the body, or at least an empty tomb being witnessed, without those women who observed the Shabbat, the idle moment in which there was neither *praxis* or communication, nor *poiesis* or creation, but sheer *theory* instead: faith desiring in the midst of emptiness. As Jan Patočka in his *Heretical Essays* said so eloquently: "…*melete thanatou*, care for death; care for the soul is inseparable from the care for death which becomes the true care for life; life (eternal) is born of this direct look at death, of an overcoming of death."[22] Again in the words of Wendell Berry:

> Unless we grieve like Mary
> at His grave, giving Him up
> as lost, no Easter morning comes.

This gazing at death, this *theoria* devoid of an object is the true and only source of life. The doctrine of *creatio ex nihilo* is precisely the affirmation of this conviction that only *theoria* can contemplate and dare to suffer by faith alone in face of nothingness.

In his long poem, called "The Book of Monastic Life," Rainer Maria Rilke approaches the emptiness of this desiring that borders on the revolt of a Job:

---

[22] Jan Patočka, *Heretical Essays in the Philosophy of History* (Chicago: Open Court, 1996), 105. Patočka was the philosophical leader of the group that wrote the Czech protest manifesto *Carta 77* to which the playwright and later president Václav Havel also belonged. Patočka died shortly after, while under what is described as police interrogation.

Your very first word was: Light:
Thus made was time. Then silent you were
     long.

Your second word became flesh
     and distress
(darkly we are submerged in his growling)
and again your face is pondering.

Yet your third
     I want not.[23]

The Word that creates, the Word that communicates entails the premonition of a third that does not come, that the poet does not want, but it is here in our midst as precisely the silence he fears and desires (*Ich aber will dein drittes nicht*), the moment of remembrance, silence, absence, and sacrifice, which we want not—yet reveals the longings of our hearts, minds, and souls where faith alone sustains us against all hope, against all love, that is, against all the flaws in our attempts of creating a better world, against all our lapses in bringing about understanding, discernment, and justice. The third the poet averts, but has it in the moment he denies it, is the sigh of the word that is just not uttered, because it simply cannot and ought not to be uttered. The "third" here is not even a word; it is a sigh, a breath that remains ineffable. Yet this sigh, this breath is also *ruach*, the very spirit of life that then does not compose a discourse, does not utter words.

---

[23] "Dein allererstes Wort war: *Licht*: / da ward die Zeit. Dann schwiegst du lange. / Dei zweites Wort ward Mensch und bange / (wir dunkeln noch in seinem Klange) / und wieder sinnt dein Angesicht. / Ich aber will dein drittes nicht." Rainer Maria Rilke, *Die Gedichte* (Frankfurt a/M: Insel, 1997), 227.

Beauty and Disturbance: Demons and Idols

Beauty, what is it if not also this sigh in face of the unspeakable and the undoable? It is not the sublime, however, for it implies shock and disturbance. Nadine Gordimer, the South African writer and anti-apartheid activist, once described the task of a writer, saying that her or his work should come upon the reader as if it were a pistol shot in the midst of a symphony. The image is drastic, shocking even, but the metaphor is fitting: the *tremendum*, the moment of awe in the otherwise predictable movements in the performance of a composition with all its sublime features and fascination. The pistol shot is the irony that breaks into analogical continuity. Its incongruity with the event, its total rupture with performance and composition is something akin to the beauty I am trying to describe, as the sigh beyond words.

In this longing and desiring that defies utterances, which remain apophatic; in this Shabbat of emptiness; in this desert of our wanting, demons haunt us and populate the void, and idols are promising us comforting ersatz presences, occupying the realm of *theoria*. Demons and idols are the biblical description of the phenomena that occupy the Shabbat by administering it and filling *theoria* with words and things.

Demonry can be described as the systemic distortion of human authentic communication and the art of discerning; it is *praxis* colonizing the Shabbat, filling that moment of sacred void with words that are not one's own. The stories of demonic possession in the Gospels, for example, are almost all described by the curious phenomenon of the incapability of the possessed to express himself or herself authentically. The possessed person is either dumb, or stutters, or else the devil speaks through him or her. To phrase in contemporary lingo, demons manifest themselves in the unexamined "isms" of the régimes of this world that occupy our existence even without ever being asked in: sexism, racism, colonialism, and so forth.

Idolatry is *poiesis* colonizing the Shabbat, filling it with labor and its products, which become fetish, fabrications, artifacts endowed with the power to arrest the gaze, to seize *theoria*, as the exemplary story of the idolatrous Golden Calf so well illustrates (Exodus 32). The people wanted a presence when Moses, the leader of the people and the prophet of YHWH, was absent. Idolatry is the intentional creation of mechanisms of oppression and domination, which turn labor into a slavery to commodities.

Both demonry and idolatry exemplify the surrender of emptiness in exchange for a presence, counterfeit as it is. Both are expressions of the failure to clearly distinguish *theoria* in its Jewish-Christian sense from either *praxis* or *poiesis*. And such lack of discernment is what often turns much of worship into a profusion of sacramentalist *poiesis* and garrulous *praxis*, and so little of prostrated *theoria*. Demonry and idolatry are stories of doing and making not because faith seeks it but because we cannot stand on faith alone while the Shabbat requires it.

This is Jewish-Christian understanding of *theoria* in a world in which we are called to create new possibilities and communicate new understandings and discernments. Yet such creation and communication can only remain as faith endeavors to allow as the moment of discontinuity and rupture in everyday life, the moment in which irony is accepted; accepted precisely on the grounds that it cannot be justified by any of the régimes of this world. It is, therefore, the breaking in of the eschatological moment into everyday life—with its rules, expectations, systems, and institutions. And this eschatological moment will not come without the trepidation of not knowing, not seeing, not being assured of whether it is the moment of condemnation or of liberation. These are the moments Walter Benjamin aptly called "chips of Messianic time…the strait gate through which the Messiah might enter."[24] Only the idle daring that is the discipline of remembrance and observance of what seems to have been gone and done for, only faithfully allowing even the past to revisit us, gestates a promise we will build on, and a love we will live by. This is faith desiring, verb intransitive.

---

[24] Benjamin, *Illuminations*, 263–64.

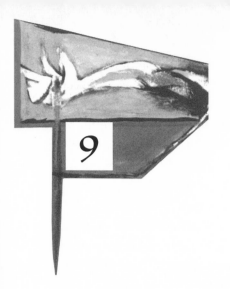

Cross and Eschatology

The Ends of the World

9

Where is tomorrow?

Peter Høeg

One of the most unexamined assumptions in the eschatological discourse of Western modernity is that it has to do with time and only time—its suspension, its consummation, or its end. Often overlooked is the relationship between eschatology and our experience of space. This silence is surprising considering that some of the most important social experiences affecting people worldwide are primordially spatial experiences—migration, homelessness, landlessness, displacement, invasion, military occupation, land confiscation, home demolition. And think about other kinds of spaces, not strictly geographical, such as social location, caste, class, economic situation. These have not received much theological treatment, revealing a deficit or a blind spot in Western theological thinking.[1]

[1] While working with landless peasants in Brazil in the 1980s, I searched in vain for theological categories to use to reflect on the very existential and pastoral subjects I encountered: millions of small farmers driven from their land, landless peasant families living for endless years in plastic tents on the sides of highways—squeezed between the traffic and the fences of under-utilized farms nearby. Since then "space," "place," and other spatial motifs have been of concern and indispensable *theologumena*. See Vítor Westhelle, "Creation Motifs in the Search for a Vital Space: A Latin American Perspective," in *Lift Every Voice: Constructing Christian Theology from the Underside*, ed. Susan Thistlethwaite and Mary Engel (San Francisco: HarperSanFrancisco, 1990), 128–287; "Re(li)gion:

144

How one can hold an eschatological vision that is not utopian, but "topic," localized—and therefore relevant to our present situation—and faithful to the biblical witness? This is the task, so let us consider some categories. Faithfulness to the biblical witness requires nothing less than trying to understand how time and space are related in writings of the Scriptures.

Time

"What is time?" "Where is tomorrow?" These are questions that Peter Høeg pursues relentlessly in his novel *Borderliners*, telling through autobiographical fiction the story of institutionalized children who did not fit in socially: borderliners! It is the question of what time means for those

The Lord of History and the Illusory Space," in *Region and Religion*, ed. Viggo Mortensen (Geneva: LWF, 1994), 79–95; "Wrappings of the Divine: Location and Vocation in Theological Perspective," *Currents in Theology and Mission* 31, no. 5 (October 2004): 368–80. Some theologians have taken up the argument and raised questions as to the appropriateness of reading eschatology in a matrix that includes a spatial dimension. Among the most receptive to attempts to connect theology and particularly eschatology to spatial experiences still reveal significant resistance to the proposal. For example. José Míguez Bonino suggests that "a Trinitarian vision of this theme [I suggested] could provide an adequate theological key" for the reconstruction of theology, but asks me if I would not be giving up the biblical eschatological vision of the future of God (José Míguez-Bonino, *Rostros del protestantismo latinoamericano* [Buenos Aires/Grand Rapids: Eerdmans, 1995], 102–4, 163 n.44. My article he discusses is "Re(li)gion: The Lord of History and the Illusory Space.") And Catherine Keller, in her book *Apocalypse Now and Then*, commends me for the same insight, but notes that I seem "all too trustful of the apocalyptic-move, indeed even translating it into the later doctrine of *creatio ex nihilo*." Such a move, she says, threatens to become "utopianized in just the sense Westhelle wishes to oppose." Instead, she suggests a "counter-apocalypse" that would "translate the notion of creation out of that absolute *origin* into that of *perpetual origination*" (Catherine Keller, *Apocalypse Now and Then* [Boston: Beacon Press, 1996], 172). Apparently I am being criticized for exactly opposite reasons: one, for not taking eschatology seriously enough, and another, for carrying it to apocalyptic extremes. In a certain sense each has recognized important points that I would like to underscore. Keller is right to point out a recurring apocalyptic theme in my text that goes against her suggestion of a "perpetual origination" and favors an argument for the significance of *creatio ex nihilo*. Earlier I have argued that in a time-space frame the apocalyptic takes on new significance that removes it far from popular images of impending catastrophe, always predicated by a temporal scheme in which space plays no role. Míguez-Bonino detects departure from a certain eschatological vision. However, I would argue that it is a departure from a Western view of history and of eschatology, but not from a biblical view of the *eschaton*, even if the former has been inscribed upon the latter.

who are on the edge of the social *space* they inhabit. The book examines and questions conceptions of linear time running across the Newtonian universe and through the inborn category of a Kantian mind. Were these the only understandings of time for the borderliners, time as a machine that nudges "out toward the edge of the abyss"?[2]

How can we think about time when we know that at its very limit time either loses its meaning or pushes us over the edge? Time has different velocities as we experience it. Time can be the ecstatic experience of a *kairos* or the relentless movement of a rhythmic *chronos*. But these are only extremes in a spectrum of countless other velocities that intersect our experiences depending on *where* we are. This language of Høeg that touches upon poetry is needed in order to detect the abstract character time has assumed in modern theological prose. Consider another novel about being at the margin; ponder the probings of Sethe, the character on the edge in Toni Morrison's novel *Beloved*:

> I was talking about time. It's so hard for me to believe in it. Some things go. Pass on. Some things just stay. I used to think it was my memory. You know. Some things you forget. Other things you never do. But it's not. Places, places are still there...not just in my rememory, but out there, in the world....I mean even if I don't think it, even if I die...[it] is still out there. Right in the place where it happened.[3]

This is the puzzle we need to work with: How does time take *place*? What is the time of salvation, of trial, of condemnation? *Where* does it happen? Or doesn't it take *place*? What do theologians say about it?

Arguably Paul Tillich is the twentieth-century theologian who has made the greatest impact on both theology *and* cultural life in the Western world. Unlike other great theological minds[4] Tillich dipped and soaked the core of his theology in the cultural milieu of the middle twentieth

---

[2] Peter Høeg, *Borderliners* (New York: Delta, 1995), 259.

[3] Toni Morrison, *Beloved* (New York: Plume, 1988), 35–36.

[4] Karl Barth or Karl Rahner might have had more impact in their respective theological traditions, Barth in Protestant theology and Rahner in Roman Catholicism, but Tillich had a greater impact in culture and religion overall.

century and learned how to read the "signs of the times" on both sides of the North Atlantic world. Unlike Barth's prescription to have the Bible in one hand and the newspaper in another, Tillich encoded the Bible into the newspaper and vice versa. He is therefore a good candidate for anyone to consult on what the West perceives as the basic challenges facing theology, and what theological agenda should be pursued.

What he saw became the explicit agenda of much of theology and, sometimes, the tacit one. The explicit agenda was the one in which his contributions were controversial within the theology of the West and therefore openly debated, like his Christology, his expressivist theory of symbol, his method of correlation, and so forth. What interests me here is to look at the tacit or implicit agenda he laid out, which was never much debated, I assume precisely because it was taken as a truism, largely self-evident and shared by the prevailing culture in the North Atlantic world.

The theologian that understood himself as being on the boundaries,[5] and used in his *Systematic Theology* and elsewhere a plethora of other spatial metaphors like dimensions, depth, limits, structure, was the same one who wrote an essay about the struggle between time and space.[6] In a typical Western binary approach, Tillich sets the two categories against each other and lined up other oppositions in which Christianity sides with time and paganism with space. The predominance of time gives rise to prophecy and monotheistic faith; space to tragedy, mysticism, and polytheism. History and the church universal are on the side of justice; the rule of space is nationalism and tribalism producing injustice; it is the victory of naturalism over the spirit, and so on. What is Tillich's motivation for debunking space from Christian theology? He is reflecting implicitly his own traumatic experience with National Socialism and its ideology of blood and soil, of Aryan purity combined with the nationalistic concept of *Lebensraum* (living or vital space). Yet, we should be reminded, abuse does not abolish the use (*abusus non tollit usus*).

---

[5] Paul Tillich, *On the Boundary: An Autobiographical Sketch* (New York: Charles Scribner's Sons, 1966).

[6] "The Struggle between Time and Space," in *Theology of Culture*, ed. Robert C. Kimball (New York: Oxford University Press, 1959), 40–51.

In spite of many metaphorical uses of space in contemporary theology, Tillich's diatribe against space and in favor of time, has received little attention in theological literature until very recently. I suspect this is not because Tillich was seen as off the mark, which he hardly ever was, either as an incisive observer of culture or as an amazingly well informed philosophical theologian. The reason is likely the opposite. He was playing a melody so much in consonance with the cultural symphony of his time *and* his place. He only formulated what was a virtual consensus: God's revelation happens in history regardless of geography.[7] That is what Michel Foucault, one of the most disturbing and incisive critics of modern Western culture, has noted. He tells an anecdote about "having been invited…by a group of architects to do a study of space…and at the end of the study someone spoke up [and]…firebombed me saying that *space* is reactionary and capitalist, but *history* and *becoming* are revolutionary."[8] Setting these categories of time and space against each other, relativity theory notwithstanding, reveals the disembedded character of our existence and its symbolic systems to describe Western modernity.

Space

In a 1975 unpublished dissertation, Eritrean theologian Yacob Tesfai raised a basic question, possibly for the first time in modern theology, regarding the adequacy of using time-bound or exclusively historical categories to interpret the biblical view of God's action and presence in the world. In "This Is My Resting Place: An Inquiry into the Role of Time and Space in the Old Testament,"[9] Tesfai criticizes modern Western biblical theology, canonized by the work of Gerhard von Rad, that God's

---

[7] Comments like the following are typical of this stance as expressed in a recent Protestant catechism, asserting that God deals with history, not primarily with nature, and as such is revealed: "Gott handelt in der Geschichte und gibt sich dadurch den Menschen zu erkennen. Mittel der Offenbarung Gottes ist also nicht in erter Linie die Natur, sonder die Geschichte." *Evangelischer Erwachsenenkatechismus* (Gütersloh: Gerd Mohn, 1975), 218.

[8] Paul Rabinow, ed., *The Foucault Reader* (New York: Pantheon, 1984), 252.

[9] Yacob Tesfai, "This Is My Resting Place: An Inquiry into the Role of Time and Space in the Old Testament," unpublished Ph.D. dissertation (Lutheran School of Theology at Chicago, 1975).

actions and revelation are to be seen as God's intervention in universal history, for which the locale is only circumstantial. Tesfai's analysis shows what recent anthropologists and philosophers have detected as a curious development in modern Western thinking: the separation of time from space. In the biblical world, says Tesfai, this would be a complete oddity. Time and space are "pocket-experiences." They are both at the same time a temporal event and spatially circumscribed at the same time. Place, locale, cannot be circumvented. God's revelation takes *place*.

What happens, happens in time because of a given space. And what literally takes place, takes place because the time is ripe. Anthony Giddens, in his book *Modernity and Self-Identity*, noted that in premodern settings "time and space were connected *through* the situatedness of place," while in modernity "the separation of time from space involved above all the development of an 'empty' dimension of time, the main lever which also pulled space away from place." And he continues: "fundamental [is] the separation of time from space for the massive dynamism that modernity introduces into human social affairs"[10]

The best illustration is the parallel and progressive divorce between the development of mechanical and then electronic clocks on one side, and Western cartography on the other. The mechanical clock inverted the causal relationship between the rotations of the Earth in relation to the Sun by representing with hands on the dial the movement of the Sun around the Earth, as was believed to be the case until Copernicus. The analogical clock established time in analogy to the Earth's rotation but without causal dependence on it (as a solar clock would have), thus we have time zones and daylight saving time. And with the digital watch late in the twentieth century, even the inverted analogy is no longer there. The day virtually breaks when the electronic alarm clock sounds.

Simultaneously, maps from the fifteenth century on became homogeneous representations of extension, loosing the connection with "situatedness" that was still present in older itineraries. Remnants of such elements of itineraries, in which sea monsters marked perceived places

---

[10] Anthony Giddens, *Modernity and Self-Identity: Self and Society in the Late Modern Age* (Stanford: Stanford University Press, 1991), 16–17.

of danger and risk, can still be found in sixteenth-century maps while modern cartography was becoming normative. These two processes, the development of mechanisms for measuring time and the homogenization of cartographic representations, move in opposite directions severing the connection between time and space, which is a common experience, but rendered unintelligible by the means available for us to represent them in a cognitive fashion.

It is no coincidence that it took an Eritrean theologian to put the bell on the neck of the theological tradition cat in accepting this modern severance between time and space. It is often a stranger who lifts up one's own idiosyncrasies. The West, since the fifteenth century, did two things: (*a*) it conquered the world geographically and intellectually, and (*b*) justified this conquering with a notion of history that regarded the adventures of Western men (*sic*) as deeds of *universal* history. In the words of Tzvetan Todorov, "'to discover' is an intransitive action."[11] Only in the sixteenth century is the verb *discover* used to describe a landfall, to account for the Portuguese and Spanish maritime explorations (and shortly thereafter, curiously and revealingly, is used by John Donne to describe a sexual encounter in his infamous poem, "To My Mistress Going to Bed"[12]).

Etymologically we might recall that the word *discover* is akin to *reveal*. Both mean to remove the veil or uncover something. Since the sixteenth century, discovery became an act of revealing something somewhere else in the world that had been veiled from European view. The discovered world became thus the parchment on which the deeds of Europeans were inscribed as acts of revelation. In the words of Karl Löwith, *Weltgeschichte* was read as *Heilsgeschehen*, world history was the register of saving events.[13] And "world" history was little more than European history. Revelation

---

[11] Tzvetan Todorov, *The Conquest of America: The Question of the Other* (New York: HarperPerennial, 1992), 13.

[12] "O my America, my new found land, / My kingdom, safeliest when with one man manned, / My mine of precious stones, my empire, / How blessed am I in this discovering thee. / To enter in these bonds is to be free, / Then where my hand is set my seal shall be." John Donne, *The Oxford Authors*, ed. John Carey (Oxford: Oxford University Press, 1990), 12–13.

[13] Karl Löwith, *Meaning in History* (Chicago: University of Chicago Press, 1964). Löwith is here elaborating on Hegel's suggestion that world history is the history of its self-consummation ("Die Weltgeschichte ist das Weltgericht").

was delivered; the apocalypse was conquered and administered. After the world had been conquered, space could no longer entail any revealing promise, hence the *eschaton* was deferred to a temporal future.

There were no limits; "discovery" became an end in itself. It made no difference what was discovered, except that it was incorporated into a historically preordained logic. Hegel gives expression to this conviction precisely after discussing the conquering of the Americas in his *Lectures on the Philosophy of History* with his famous statement: "Europe is definitely [*schlechthin*] the end of world history."[14] Schleiermacher, Hegel's colleague and foe at the University of Berlin in the beginning of the nineteenth century, shared this in common with the philosopher. Arguing that there are no new heresies, for since antiquity Christianity was no longer challenged or infiltrated by other religious ideas, Schleiermacher shows that the missionary efforts of the church followed the same pattern of "discovery." Since there are no longer any limits, there is no possible transgression.[15] Where heresy is no longer possible, novelty is also an impossibility. The word *heresy* etymologically means "a choice," "an option," or "being set apart," but it can also mean "conquest," "capture." The irony in this is that the European or Western "conquering" of the world, the great "heresy," became the norm from which no deviation would be possible, no "anti-heresy" would be allowed. Heresy became absolute, normative. Spatially the *eschaton* had been reached. The only meaning left to assign the word was an exclusive temporal meaning.[16]

---

[14] Georg Wilhelm Friedrich Hegel, *Werke* (Frankfurt a/M: Suhrkam, 1970), 12:134.

[15] One needs a limit to be able to transgress, a beyond to trespass. What others thought or believed did not make any difference, for Christianity became the universal name for religion in its purest positive manifestation. In these circumstances, Schleiermacher writes, "...new heresies no longer arise, now that the Church recruits itself out of its own resources; and the influence of alien faiths on the frontier and the mission-field of the Church must be reckoned at zero." Friedrich Schleiermacher, *The Christian Faith* (Edinburgh: T&T Clark, 1989), 96.

[16] Outer space, however, still remains charged with eschatological imagery. But earthly, social space no longer does.

Sacred Spaces?

Does this all mean a desacralization or profanization of all spaces, locales, things, and bodies? No! In fact, the very opposite is the case. Columbus's case is here telling. His justification for conquering and plundering of the New World was that it was done for the sake of amassing the resources to launch a crusade to conquer the Holy House of Jerusalem.[17] Sacred spaces and sacred things were now understood within this same story in which time and space are held apart. Sacred spaces, like chastity, are hardly more than markers to define by default what can be plundered and raped. A sacred thing is a cipher for all the rest that is disposable or is deemed disposable. The former is protected from time while the latter is only a function of it. As long as we have sacred things, sacred places, dissociated from their epiphanic time—geography without genealogy—we will have never-ending dump sites and places or bodies to be violated.

Take, for example, the studies of Mircea Eliade on *The Sacred and the Profane*.[18] The distinction, he shows, emerges from the analysis of societies that demarcated their cosmos from the unknown territories and societies at its margins, the chaotic. But something happens once there is no longer the mysterious "beyond" in space, when the whole world has been colonized. (Actually, the true continuation of the ancient distinction between cosmos and chaos now has to be located in our fascination and awe attached to extraterrestrial speculations.) The homogenization of the Earth came as a result of the establishment of its spherical nature and the actual conquering of it through navigation since the fifteenth century. The chaotic, the uncanny was cosmicized. Since then, the profane is separated from the sacred by an abstract act of the mind that sets those spaces, the sacred and the profane, against each other. There was always the holy, the sacred, but it was defined by the religious experience as such; it was the predicate of a hierophany and unlike now, its presupposition. It was only with Schleiermacher's *Speeches* (1799), Durkheim's *Elementary Forms of*

---

[17] 26 December 1492, *Diario de Colón* (Madrid: Cultura Hispanica, 1968), 139. Notice that this intention of Columbus, as Hegel makes reference to it early in the nineteenth century was well known and celebrated in Europe (Hegel, *Werke* 12:490).

[18] Mircea Eliade, *The Sacred and the Profane* (New York: Harvest, 1959), 29–32.

Religious Life (1912), and Otto's *The Idea of the Holy* (1923) that the *idea* of "the holy" defined religious experiences and, therefore, also whatever was deemed profane.[19] These categories did not exist before apart from an event that was not essentially tied a priori to a given space. In other words, the *idea* of the holy, of the sacred, and the *idea* of the profane is quite a recent creation.

Eschatology

It is in this context that eschatology as the doctrine of the last "things" becomes the teachings about the last times or of a decisive time, either in a millennialist sense of a time set in the calendar for the end of the world, or as an eternal present, a "kairotic" dormant possibility slumbering beneath the tick-tock of the clock of history.[20] Whether present, future, realized, inaugurated, kairotic, proleptic, consequent, or whatever interpretation eschatology has received, it has been purged from the disturbing undecidability of the biblical view of the eschaton. The word in Greek can mean something that happens in time, but it can equally and simultaneously describe rank, the last in a series, as it can also be descriptive of the outer limits of a place. When we translate the term it receives now a single, decided meaning referring either to a place or to a time. But even when the context suggests one meaning, like "being witnesses...to the end of the world" (*heos eschatou tes ges*) (Acts 1:8), which in our translations normally receives an exclusive geographical acceptation, in the ears of the early Christians it very likely also suggested something that could be equally well translated as "until the end of the earth," suggesting a temporal acceptation also supported by the particle *hoes*, which can equally indicate a temporal as well as a spatial limit. It is only we who need to think either/or. Pedro Casaldáliga, Brazilian bishop, poet, and theologian,

---

[19] Art. "Heilig," in *Die Religion in Geschichte und Gegenwart*, 3rd ed. (Tübingen: J. C. B.Mohr [Paul Siebeck], 1959), 3:146–55.

[20] With these words Bultmann closes the Gifford Lectures 1955: "Always in your present lies the meaning in history, and you cannot see it as spectator, but only in your responsible decisions. In every moment slumbers the possibility of being the eschatological moment. You must awaken it." Rudolf Bultmann, *The Presence of Eternity: History and Eschatology* (New York: Harper & Brothers, 1957), 155.

expressed this in the following terms, explaining that the task of the church as the sacrament of the world is to pay attention to places: "the 'signs of the times' had to be complemented with the 'signs of places'."[21] Or, as one of his aphorisms states: "The Universal Word speaks dialect."[22]

Can we step outside of the modern Western predicament of thinking into this binary exclusion of time and space? Do we realize that the time of judgment comes always in a place of trial? The temptation here, of course, is to fall back into the binary opposition and just revert the axiological values and say that space is good and time is bad. But this would be nothing else than reinstating exactly the same problem. How can we think differently, not in a different way *we* might be able to think, but thinking differently by way of an *other*, or "thinking through others"?[23]

Cross

There is no theo-*logy* of the cross; at least not in the sense of being a disciplined, systematic and organized discourse about the cross and Christ's passion. The cross is the crucial point in time and space in which an exit, a way out seems not to be available—yet somehow it is there like the ineffable Shabbat. Not knowing how to express it or name it, should we keep trying? Language fails us. And yet we must speak; we must transgress the impossibility of language once Shabbat is over.

This transgression of language is an apocalyptic gesture in the way we have been using the word *apocalyptic* here: not as a literary genre, but rather to designate the precise sense of an ethos conveying this crossing of time *and* space in which there is this simultaneous coincidence, a clenching, a conflation of opposites (what Nicolas of Cusa called *coincidentia oppositorum*), of affirmation and denial, of disclosure and concealment, of presence and absence. It is not a moment of transition, an opportunity for a syllogism, but the denial of all mediations, in which the experience of

[21] Pedro Casaldáliga. *Creio na Justiça e na Esperança* (Rio de Janeiro: Civ. Brasileira, 1978), 211.

[22] Cited by Hermann Brandt, *Gottes Gegenwart in Lateinamerika* (Hamburg: Steinmann & Steinmann, 1992), 134.

[23] See Richard A. Shweder, *Thinking through Cultures: Expeditions in Cultural Psychology* (Cambridge: Harvard University Press, 1991), 108–10.

both, the end of the aeon and the beginning of it, are so imminent that it suspends all transaction, all economy. The Latin equivalent of the Greek *apokalypsis*, *revelatio* (hence the English "revelation") conveys this. In one sense it is an unveiling, a laying bare, but the prefix (*re-* in Latin, or *apo-* in Greek) reserves some surprises in the undecidability of its meaning. It can be the removal of the veil but it can also means something else, the moving-away-from the veil so as to make it even more veiling, or even double veiling. The text from Melito of Sardis[24] shows this meaning well when the naked God, the utterly revealed God, is simultaneously the one on which the light no longer shines. The totally visible, exposed, and stripped God (what Luther called the *deus nudus*) is in the utter darkness in the middle of the day.

The apostle Paul, groping for language to express this impossibility, which he himself called the "apocalypse of Jesus Christ" (1 Cor. 1:7), could only express it in paradoxical terms pairing notions such as "foolishness and wisdom," "weakness and power," "noble and low."[25] He composed in the opening of the First Letter to the Corinthians a text that is both striking insofar as its boldness in language is concerned, but helpless insofar as any systematic effort tries to put order into his language and clear the meaning of its semantics. Luther would be another example. How should we read *ad deum contra deum confungere* ("to flee from [God] and find refuge in God against God") if not in this undecidable apocalyptic verve?[26]

The term *apocalyptic* names, then, the literal meaning of the death of God in the cross of Jesus, and in a metaphorical sense designates our little, small, or weak apocalypses in so far as the former, the literal meaning,

---

[24] "He that hung up the earth *in space* was *Himself* hanged up; He that fixed the heavens was fixed *with nails*; He that bore up the earth was borne up on a tree; the Lord *of all* was subject to ignominy in a naked body—God put to death! The King of Israel slain with Israel's right hand! Alas for the new wickedness of the new murder! The Lord was exposed with naked body: He was not deemed worthy even of covering; and, in order that He might not be seen, the luminaries turned away, and the day became darkened, because they slew God, who hung naked on the tree." Melito of Sardis, *Ante-Nicene Fathers* (Peabody, Mass.: Hendrickson, 1994), 8:757b.

[25] Alexandra R. Brown, *The Cross and Human Transformation: Paul's Apocalyptic Word in 1 Corinthians* (Minneapolis: Fortress, 1995), 76, lists sixteen pairs of antithetical formulations Paul uses in 1 Corinthians 1:28—2:5.

[26] *WA* 5.204, 26f.

sheds light into, or offers an impossible language, to the understanding of our own experience of limits, of being at the edge of the abyss. The literal and the metaphorical meanings are not the same, yet they share the same linguistic impossibility. The cross of Jesus, in the words of Mary Solberg, represents an "epistemological break" with the ways we organize our knowledge of the world.[27]

Liminality

A spatial concern, the lifting up of the importance of locale, of place, is theologically speaking, not a concern for the celebration of places, a theological version of a Sierra Club calendar, the crowning of a theology of geography to outdo a theology of history. The spatial quest is decisive insofar as it is a quest for the limit, the borderline, the frontier, the margin, the horizon, the divide—words that define a place that is no-place, for it is not only the limit of a space, but a limit intersected by a time that is equally evasive; a time of ending that is no-time, but simultaneously the time of coming (*ad-ventus*) that also fails to be measured, chronometered; for what comes does not come *in* time, instead it comes *on* or *upon* time. What the cross does is precisely this reorientation of our gaze to the limits, the *eschata*. What it reveals is exactly the apocalypse, which is revelation, and at once its very concealment; a revelation hidden in its opposite (*revelatio abscondita sub contraria specie*), as Luther said in trying his hand at explaining the apocalypse of God in Jesus of Nazareth.

In an influential essay that Ernst Käsemann published some decades ago, he claimed that "the apocalyptic was the mother of all Christian theology."[28] Käsemann argues that the apocalyptic, as a specific kind of

---

[27] Mary Solberg, *Compelling Knowledge: A Feminist Proposal for an Epistemology of the Cross* (Albany: SUNY Press, 1997).

[28] Ernst Käsemann, "Die Anfänge christlicher Theologie," in *Exegetische Versuche und Besinnungen* (Göttingen: Vandenhoeck and Ruprecht, 1964), 2:100.

religious eschatology, was the dominant frame within which early Christian theology unfolded itself and received a distinctive character.[29] The apocalyptically framed eschatology recognized that God's revelation, the "apocalypse of Jesus Christ" (Gal. 1:12), happens in a moment of profound crisis that marks a point of reversal, in which things are turned upside down; what appears to be the case is, in God's incoming kingdom, really its reverse. And such was that moment, and the cross of Jesus stood at the hinge of the turning. For the apocalyptic, the *eschaton*, is not just an end to be reached, a telos. It is better described as a margin that marks the critical turning point of transition and the axis of inversion from one state to the other that, according to Paul, has already broken in with the cross of Christ.[30] As a crucial time, it entails the moment in which the end is at the same time the beginning, the last are the first and the first last, the rich are the poor and poor rich, life is death and death is life, the blessed are cursed and those who are cursed blessed, and everything is inverted. This historical reversal brings about a transvaluation of all values. Consider the words of the Magnificat of Luke 1:52-53: "He brought down the powerful from their thrones, and lifted up the lowly; he has filled the hungry with good things, and sent the rich away empty."

To keep the gaze at that unseemly spectacle is what the apostles, so reluctantly, had to learn. It is the uncanny, the unbearable vision. If it is all too familiar to us, we might have not been there "when they crucified my Lord," yet we have experienced it in every moment we run into the limits of the spaces we inhabit, the borders of our geographies. And they are legion. We know them as much as we avoid and dread them. For example, there is a psychological geography, the terrain of our gathered self, that has its limits, the point in which the self collapses. There is the geography

---

[29] Käsemann actually claims that, more than frame, the apocalyptic is the source of Christian theology. He has been criticized for the reductionistic character of his thesis. But even if the radical thesis that holds a causal link between the apocalyptic and Christian theology has been challenged, the contextual argument of Käsemann still holds if, instead of source ("mother"), we use it as context. See also Käsemann's defense of his argument against critics in "Zum Thema der urchristlicher Apokalyptik," in *Exegetische Versuche und Besinnungen*, 2:105–31.

[30] Brown, *The Cross and Human Transformation*, 13 n.1.

of our body that is delimited by the point it "reveals" its dysfunction, a condition that invites our constant denial, or else threatens to turn us into hypochondriacs. And so there are ethnic, racial, social, cultural, political, economic, geopolitical, and so many other geographies that lay bare the apocalypses; the limits of the homely, the familiar, that which centers our spaces. They are often not more than small apocalypses whose "weak messianic power" (Walter Benjamin) are yet strong enough to awaken in us the onslaught of the uncanny, the unfamiliar, the *Unheimlich*.

Yet, the apocalyptic message wants to convey precisely this paradox: it is at the end that a beginning is possible, it is death that brings about life, it is the awful that is also awesome, the *tremendum* is the *fascinans*. As Hölderlin says and I have previously mentioned, it is where danger lies that liberation comes from,[31] but do we want to be saved? Or do we long, rather, to be safe? Is this not the message, the lesson that we learn from that other apocalypse, the apocalypse of Jesus Christ? Between that and ours there is a trail that is marked by the blood of those who have witnessed, have been martyrs (the very word we translate as "witness"), not only because they confessed Jesus, but because they themselves stood at the borderline of their own familiar, because they had learned to keep the gaze steady and read their own apocalypse in the light and the darkness of that other one to whom they attested. Martyrs are needed because only they, from Stephen to Don Oscar Romero, can show us the way back to that one apocalypse that reorients us and allows us to read the signs of times and places, facing the uncanny filled with hope—but which is a hope against all hope.

Dietrich Bonhoeffer called this the cost of discipleship. But if this is its cost who can be saved? How many, say, tenured professors, have left, are leaving, or are ready to leave safety behind in order to be saved? The uncanny, the apocalyptic obfuscating light and blinding darkness, the *Unheimlich*, this limiting space and time that is at once no-space and no-time is not wide enough for all of us to inhabit at once, in the unlikely case we would opt for it. We have been spared and our weak apocalypses

---

[31] "Nah ist / Und schwer zu fassen der Gott / Wo aber Gefahr ist, wächst / Das Rettende auch." Friedrich Hölderlin, *Gedichte/Hyperion* (Augsburg: Wilhelm Goldmann, 1978), 138.

don't amount most of the time to a situation without remedy. We have insurance policies and psychoanalysts, community organizers and drugs, racism workshops and families, political treaties and labs, street rallies and churches, not-for-profit organizations and Sunday brunches, self-care techniques and committees, this and that, mediating detours that have spared us from or circumvented our small apocalypses; they do alleviate and buffer the effect, the conflation that apocalypses produce. There is home, at least for many of us.

Home

Many have been spared, not yet saved, but spared. But at what cost? Whose blood has spared our own shedding? Whose crosses have sent us to the coziness of a home?

There is a theorem of sorts attributed to Justin Martyr that attempts to "demonstrate" logically that the greater the number of Christian martyrs forced into the arena, the exponentially greater number of other Christians would be spared. Literary critic and philosopher René Girard earned his fame by popularizing this theorem in what he called the "scapegoat" theory, according to which every society, in order to relieve potentially annihilating internal strife, singles out scapegoats that embody in themselves and thus represent the causes of the contentious enmity, and therefore, by their sacrifice, relieve society from the consequences of an open confrontation of all against all.[32] But is that what we can conclude, that we have been spared only to be then finally condemned, like a death-row inmate being treated for an illness so that she might, in good health, reach the day of her execution? Where is grace in this apparently unavoidable calculus of a proportional relation between sacrifice and safety? How do we get across the apocalyptic Rubicon to see a glorious new day, while we are being spared? Can we be saved, can we enjoy the hour and the place of a new creation, the glory of the *fascinans* in the face of a wonderful new creation, and the uncanny *tremendum* of an empty tomb?

---

[32] René Girard, *Violence and the Sacred* (Baltimore: John Hopkins University Press, 1977).

The Stations of the Cross Revisited

Via Crucis et Resurrectionis

10

A cross is a blunt and graceless form. It has not the completeness and satisfying quality of a circle. It does not have the grace of a parabola or the promise of a long curve....A cross speaks not of unity but of brokenness, not of harmony but ambiguity; it is a form of tension and not of rest....The cross is the symbol because the whacks of life take that shape....And unless you have a crucified God, you don't have a big enough God.

Joseph Sittler

In the Middle Ages the Franciscans introduced a spiritual exercise that has remained very popular up to present-day Catholicism and has been adopted in some Protestant circles. It is called variously *via crucis*, *via sacra*, the *via dolorosa*, or the Stations of the Cross. Traditionally, there are fourteen stations that begin with the condemnation by Pilate and continue through the burial of Jesus in the tomb. Each station registers one of the events described in the Gospels, from Jesus' condemnation through his death.[1] It is a vivid reminder of the passion of Jesus.

The exercise of walking through the stations while meditating on the meaning of each station has become a powerful exercise of piety. It is sometimes presented in such a way that the suffering of the people of a particular community fills the content of each station, that is, the conditions under which the people and their struggle are each associated with one of the stations, turning the suffering of Christ on his way to the cross into a template for the suffering of the people.

---

[1] There have been both an insertion of a fifteenth stage—the finding of the cross by St. Helena, mother of Constantine—and also reductions. See the article, "Stations of the Cross," in *New Catholic Encyclopedia*, 2nd ed. (Farmington Hills, Mich.: The Catholic University of America/Gale, 2002).

Dolorism or Resurrectionism

The *via dolorosa* ends, in its traditional form, at the point where Jesus' body is laid in the tomb. The stations are displayed, within a church nave or garden, in a circular pattern with the fourteenth station, the laying of the body in the tomb, normally followed by the first one, the condemnation by Pilate. This pattern does not include the resurrection nor does it send us to shabbat rest and observance; it suggests a constant circular motion through the passion in which the last step sends us back to the beginning in an unending morbid dance, a choreography of agony. Although those who follow the exercise do not always reflect a morbid attitude, it is hard to articulate its full significance without reducing the circular reenactment of the way to the cross to an attitude that turns to evil banality in endless ritual reenactment.

We might concede that this effacement of the resurrection has some merit in a North American setting, especially if Douglas John Hall is correct in his diagnosis of an official optimism syndrome that leads to what he names "resurrectionism."[2] In other cultural contexts, however, such as Latin America, where this spiritual exercise is very popular, the opposite is true. In Latin America Good Friday is not followed by any Easter, according to Guatemalan Angel Miguel Asturias, the Nobel Prize winner for literature. Peruvian writer Manuel Scorza says that in Latin America there are five seasons: Spring, Summer, Fall, Winter, and Massacre. In this context, the popular *via crucis* can easily turn into a piety described as *dolorismo*, a mystifying devotion to suffering and pain, often coupled with fatalism. What is the place of the resurrection in the context of a theology of the cross that does not run too fast from the cross only to fall into "resurrectionism"? Or, what is the role of the resurrection in a theology that ends up in masochistic praise of suffering, in fatalism or *dolorismo*?

---

[2] Douglas John Hall, *Professing the Faith: Christian Theology in a North American Context* (Minneapolis: Fortress Press, 1993), 528.

Theories of Resurrection

Paul Tillich finds three meanings attached to "resurrection" that can be discretely examined. He calls them "theories."[3] The first is the *physical* theory: a body that has been dead is actually raised up to life with its physical and biological characteristics restored. The second is a *spiritual* meaning for resurrection in which the community, empowered by the Spirit, raises Jesus into the *kerygma*, into the proclamation of his spiritual presence. The resurrection in this second case is the transformation of the proclaimer into the one who is proclaimed. In popular spirituality the resurrection is deliverance from the finitude of the flesh, while in academic theologies resurrection is used to indicate the power of the message of Jesus, which lifts up his followers; Christ resurrects into the believing community. The third meaning for Tillich is the *psychological* one, which interprets the resurrection as an event that takes place in the mind of the one who experiences it. Resurrection is the individual's capability of seeing beyond the tragic dimensions of life and living in this hope unencumbered by physical and social constraints.

Since the emergence of liberation theologies, a fourth distinct meaning has been added to those Tillich discerned. In this meaning a *social or corporate* understanding of resurrection has been proposed; the resurrection is connected to the overcoming of oppressive social structures. Resurrection and insurrection overlap. (It is wrong, however, to assume that in liberation theology the former is reduced to the latter.) Resurrection in the sense of insurrection is seen as a process still unfolding itself, overcoming *barriers* of time and space to which the symbol of death refers.

These different interpretations are not mutually exclusive; we can find them all displayed in the New Testament. The physical event appears mostly in the Synoptic Gospels. Paul employs both the spiritual and the psychological interpretations. The paschal tradition's celebration of the resurrection, an analogy to the passage through the sea into the land

---

[3] See Paul Tillich, *Systematic Theology*, 3 vols. (Chicago: University of Chicago Press, 1951–1963) 2:155–56.

of promise, represents the fourth meaning. The temptation for Western rational thought is to surrender the physical interpretation since it is the least plausible by our canons of rationality. The other three can be systematized more easily. The resurrection of the body would remain only as a metaphor.[4] But it is precisely the way it disturbs rationality that makes so appealing the accounts of the empty tomb and the physical appearance of Jesus with the scars of death in his body.

Instead of a metaphor, which is still ruled by analogy and correspondence, another trope can be suggested: a cipher, in the sense of a code-sign given as a token. In itself the cipher's meaning is negligible, but it entails an encoded message whose meaning is concealed, with the deferred promise that its supporting evidence is found elsewhere. Consider, for example, a cipher in a text, like a numeric reference or an asterisk that tells us that the argument made here relies on information that is not established in the main text itself. The cipher pledges that the supporting evidence is elsewhere, outside of the text in which it appears and to which it points. And suppose that this supporting evidence is not immediately available; it will take a time-consuming effort to locate it. Now, extend the simile and imagine that the evidence is not yet actually available anywhere or reachable. In this case one has to accept or reject the argument at face value while waiting for the evidence to surface or for one's mind to change.

I suggest the cipher as an allegory for the relationship between our canons of truth and knowledge and the accounts of the resurrection event. What is not available is not available because it does not fall within the canons of rationality that we presently accept as the ruling régime of truth. But it might be accepted in another régime. I will illustrate with a recent case in point. Half a century ago Western medicine unanimously rejected the therapeutic effectiveness of acupuncture. It was considered "alternative" at best, pure quackery by most. With development of neurobiology in the West, however, it was learned that acupuncture does indeed have therapeutic properties, the conclusion reached by the same standards of

---

[4] Even Wolfhart Pannenberg, who has made the strongest case in recent theology for the historicity of the resurrection, concedes that ultimately we are talking about a metaphor, an "absolute metaphor" but still a metaphor. See his *Jesus—God and Man* (Philadelphia: Westminster, 1974), 187, and also *Basic Questions*, vol. 1 (London: SCM, 1970), 236 and footnote.

Western medicine that had thoroughly rejected it. It took what philosopher of science Thomas Kuhn called a paradigm shift for this "knowledge," not previously accepted as legitimate, to be recognized.[5] The resurrection is such an event; it invites us to recognize, before anything else, that we cannot think about it reasonably because of the limits we set and accept about what can be discerned. Even more provocatively, Michel Foucault would say, "each society has its regime of truth, its 'general politics' of truth....Truth is linked in a circular relation with systems of power which produce and sustain it, and to effects of power which it induces and which extends it."[6]

The resurrection is then a reminder to us that what we cannot reasonably think through could very well be the fault of the limits of our rationality, and the approach to what it entails should be an invitation to transgress these limits and probe other knowledges. Our suggestion earlier that resurrection be approached as a practice is directed against these "theoretical" framings of the event. It is a practice of labor, of mourning, and of love that moves beyond and across the limits of the régimes of truth to which we are beholden.

This seems to be the decisive factor for maintaining the connection between the cross and the resurrection. It means that however we might interpret the resurrection, it is above all an active engagement with cross and suffering, a care for death. What is this care, this practice that goes against the rules of our economies? If the resurrection sends us beyond our conventional ways of reasoning, then whatever happens in the cross is cast in this same light; what we see is hidden under its opposite. This is what brings us to revisit the tradition of the Stations of the Cross, for there we find a particular attitude displayed. In the face of suffering, cross, and death, what does one do? The answer of the Stations is, first, there is care, and there is also an itinerary we need to follow. The meaning of this care was examined earlier under the notion of *theoria* as Shabbat. The itinerary was described as a practice of resurrection, but the "plan" of the itinerary remains to be addressed.

---

[5] Thomas Kuhn, *The Structure of Scientific Revolutions* (Chicago: University of Chicago Press, 1962).
[6] Paul Rabinow, ed., *The Foucault Reader* (New York: Pantheon, 1984), 73–74.

Maps and Itineraries

I am using the notion of "itinerary" in opposition to "map." A map is a representation of a given topographical reality, characterized by a homogeneous representation of a territory. In a map there is no privileged space. In it one has the freedom to select spaces and decide to locate oneself here or there by the move of a finger. There is no privileged space; all is flat. Maps are also neutral. To move in a map from A to B one might choose an innumerable selection of courses. Modern cartography emerged precisely when the European conquest of the world began in the fifteenth century, when places were no longer qualified by given entities (such as sea monsters and the like), which singled out privileged spaces and locales; now all could be mapped and distances quantified, and thus explored and conquered. A map gives one the options and the means to go where one chooses but does not tell us in advance where to go or the course to take. Explorers are the masters of their own destiny. Maps are ways of detecting a reality for the sake of its exploration; they have no teleology, no intrinsic destination.

An itinerary is different; it has implications! It elects a privileged, valued place to go and then tells one how to get there. Itineraries are like a child's treasure hunt. It tells the steps to take, the direction to follow, and the turns required at certain points in order to reach the goal. Subway plans are a modern equivalent. They tell you where you are and what to do in order to reach your destination in the most efficient way. Other factors do not count. The territory, the geographic incidents, the urban surroundings or the landscape do not matter. Itineraries, unlike maps, are always goal directed in nature, they focus on the journey and its envisioned end; itineraries are about praxis. Theologically speaking, itineraries are maps in a practico-eschatological perspective, maps are itineraries without eschatology, without any set telos, without implying a praxis.

Two things are required in advance of using an itinerary: one needs to locate where one is and know where one is going, point of departure and destination. In this way the Stations of the Cross or *via crucis* is an itinerary: undertaking the *via crucis*, one meditates at each station, trying to place oneself in Jesus' position or to find ourselves or our communities represented in that station. When this is done, one knows to move to the next station or goal and on this way to the end. Inspired by this traditional practice of Franciscan piety and considering the different perspectives from which one can look at the cross and experience it, we can devise a similar itinerary—one that does not end with the laying of the body in the tomb.

A cautionary note is here in place. An itinerary might turn into a ready-made scheme that tends to "naturalize," to produce a logically predictable rationality that pretends to have the "know-how" of a given journey. This certainly would betray the constant epistemological break that the cross imposes upon any rationality. Nonetheless, aware of this risk, our search for meaning, however fragmentary, requires a certain amount of systematization in the utter recognition of having to leave it behind in the moment we start to feel comfortable with it, in the moment in which the uncanny is domesticated, the *tremendum* is administered. But not to do it would be to surrender to irrationalism or cynicism. We are still asked to be ready to give reasons (*apologien*) for the hope that is in us (1 Peter 3:15).

An Interlude: Toni Morrison's *Beloved*

Before I propose this experiment let us consider an example. It is from Toni Morrison's awesomely disturbing and eloquently elegant book, *Beloved*.[7] The whole book offers an intricate argument, full of nuances, but it is blunt enough not to fall down in common places. I bring this book into consideration to lift up some of the crucial moves made by the author in structuring the narrative. The result could be described as a fictional commentary on the relationship between cross and resurrection. Morrison's book tells the story of Sethe, a slave woman running from capture who, in an act of despair at the fear of her child being returned with her to slavery, cuts the throat of her baby daughter. Later she finally escapes from the south while pregnant with another child to whom she gives birth during her flight. This daughter, Denver, takes the place of the

---

[7] Toni Morrison, *Beloved* (New York: Plume, 1987).

baby she murdered to save her from the fate of a life of slavery that she had endured for too long.

Sethe's life is a labor of mourning for the lost child and of devotion for the one she kept, until one day when, out of nowhere, a girl shows up at the front steps of her house. It does not take long for that girl to upset Sethe's whole existence, her man and her daughter. The girl brings light and joy to their lives but also a very scary sense of the uncanny, until Sethe realizes that for her this mysterious girl is her own beloved child, the one she left behind as dead. At this realization all Sethe's joy turns into obsession to keep her beloved, to posses her, the one she had presumably murdered. In this obsession and disordered depression, Sethe loses her job and ends up more and more derelict with only her obsession to retain her lost daughter. One day Beloved, the child left behind as dead, now pregnant herself, leaves home not to return again. Melancholy sets in and Sethe, in depression and a double share of mourning, will not leave her bed. Her man, who left when he realized that Sethe had closed herself to the world and to people around her in her obsession with the girl she took to be her daughter, now returns to take care of her to restore to health her damaged life.

Movements of reversal happen at many levels, but there are two trajectories in which these reversals take place that organize the structure of the narrative. One is a historical or diachronic movement that encompasses transitions between slavery and freedom, mourning and joy, south and north, shame and pride, fear and courage, struggle and peace, death and life. At another level, crossing the first one in a synchronic transaction, is the movement of reversals—what seems to be the case, the manifest side, reverts itself in a concealed side. A brutal crime conceals an act of supreme love, an absence is filled with a constant sense of presence, a return conceals a true departure.

The Itinerary of Cross *and* Resurrection

These two axes in Morrison's novel, the diachronic and the synchronic, obey a certain rhythm; they have a choreography, a certain movement that might exemplify the relationship between the cross and resurrection.

The pattern of the simultaneous movements along the two axes serves as a matrix that, with the help of some biblical passages, will allow us to distinguish some "stations" in the movement from life to cross to resurrection. Unlike the Stations of the Cross, in this case the movement is not restricted to the passion narrative, but encompasses the relationship of life, passion, death, and resurrection as narrated by the Gospels. It forms, rather, a permanent movement of both experience and interpretation that allows us to identify where we stand and what is being required of us if we find ourselves in one of those given moments. The itinerary has a horizontal "8" shape comprised of four stations. In the diachronic movement it goes from Good Friday to Easter, from life to death and from death to life. In the synchronic dimension it moves from what is manifest to what is concealed and from the concealed to the manifest. When the movement stops, when one is paralyzed in a given position—that is when we can diagnose certain forms of problematic expressions of both a theology of the cross and belief in the resurrection that have been already discussed. These are then the "stations," four steps in a dance that often is immobilized, frozen in the midst of motion.

The Cross Manifest

> Not only did she have to live out her years in a house palsied by the baby's fury for having her throat cut, but…those ten minutes were longer than life, more alive, more pulsating than the baby's blood that soaked her fingers like oil.[8]

The manifest side of the cross can be expressed by the experience of pain and suffering. It is the visible side of the crucifixion, the throbbing insidiousness of violence. To stay caught at this station leads to what has been called *dolorismo*, the mystifying, even masochistic glorification of suffering. The text of Mark 15:6-15 that presents the people crying out for Jesus to be crucified represents the mechanism of this mystification: suffering and sacrifice of oneself or of another are ways of reproducing a scapegoat

---

[8] Ibid., 5.

mechanism through which we try to divert attention from the need to address implicit violence and injustices. Suffering in itself then becomes expiatory.

Atonement doctrines are often caught in this mechanism of surrogacy. As René Girard points out, such mechanisms of surrogacy are particularly prominent in communities that have suffered violence: "any community that has fallen prey to violence or has been stricken by some overwhelming catastrophe hurls itself blindly into the search for a scapegoat."[9] Jesus in his cross is the scapegoat. He is pollution itself, or as Paul says, he was made to be sin (2 Cor. 5:21). Obviously, there is a difference between the overt hatred toward the scapegoat and the pious devotion to cross and suffering. They are essentially the same, however. Once the violence is perpetrated and the community relieved from the overt anger caused by the violence that threatens it, the one who was the object of hatred is transformed in an object of devotion. This is how surrogacy operates. And the same process that finds an external victim for sacrifice can also be internalized. In this case one's own endured suffering is endured because it also releases oneself from the costly need to respond to the violence. This is a common phenomenon observed in societies that have been exposed to violence and colonialism. Therefore, it has been named *dolorism*, the mystification and sublimation of pain (*dolor*) and suffering.

> It was as though Sethe didn't really want forgiveness given; she wanted it refused. And Beloved helped her out.[10]

The Cross Concealed

> This and much more Denver heard her say from her corner chair, trying to persuade Beloved, the one and only person she felt she had to convince, that what she had done was right because it came from true love.[11]

---

[9] René Girard, *Violence and the Sacred* (Baltimore: Johns Hopkins University Press, 1977), 79.
[10] Morrison, *Beloved*, 252.
[11] Ibid.

To avoid our getting trapped in *dolorism*, the manifest side of the cross must move us to its concealed side, symbolically represented by the tomb, the place where suffering is hidden. In this concealment the cross calls us to this labor of mourning and love, of addressing the pain and, appeased, like in the need to relinquish, to let it go. It takes this gesture that in love brings us to the place where we might finally say, "it is over," and be ready for new surprises. Exemplified by the interesting story of the women over-come by terror (Mark 16:1-8) at finding the tomb empty and hearing that Jesus had risen, we don't want to be surprised, disturbed, or upset in the way our expectations have prepared us to face fate.

Here the temptation is to be frozen in defeatism. We put so much energy into coping with tragedy, we don't want the tomb to be empty. We want a body we can see when it is buried, and then we can just give up. There is a profound sadness in those mourning women but also a sense of expectation. As they approach, the question on their minds was, Who will roll aside the stone that covers the entrance to the tomb? It would be their job and their pride. They would find a way. But the stone had been already rolled, and they felt scared and useless; all their preparation, all their mechanisms for coping with tragedy had been upset. What of all that labor of mourning? It is easier to administer sorrow than have it replaced by a surprise that is beyond our control.[12]

---

[12] The rolling of the stone evokes an interesting comparison with the classic myth of Sisyphus, who was condemned in the underworld to role a stone uphill, but once the top of the hill was reached the stone would roll back down; Sisyphus had to return and role the stone again unceasingly. A fascinating analysis of this myth by Albert Camus presents the story of someone who defies a fate that is unavoidable by administering it as if it were on his terms: "Sisyphus teaches us a superior happiness that negates the gods and raises rocks." When Sisyphus comes down the mountain to get his rock back, says Camus, his face does not convey despair or distress: "One must imagine Sisyphus happy" (Albert Camus, *The Myth of Sisyphus and Other Essays* [New York: Vintage, 1955], 88–91). Like the women at the tomb, if the stone suddenly remained unmovable in the unstable pick at the top of the mountain, Sisyphus too would feel useless and scared about a fate that can no longer be predicted and has fallen outside of his "control." Camus's fateful existentialism is in fact a commentary on fatalism. And fatalism is to be immobilized at the concealed facet of the cross and just say: that is the way it is.

You forgot to smile / I loved you / You hurt me / You came back to me / You left me.[13]

The Resurrection Manifest

[He] went off with two buckets to a place near the river's edge that only he knew about where blackberries grew, tasting so good and happy that to eat them was like being in church.[14]

The concealed side of the cross must move us in hope to see that there is a transformative power at work even in the midst of a total defeat, a power creating even out of nothing. A corpse is risen and it is attested as the "pledge" (*arrabon*) (2 Cor. 1:22), or "first fruit" (*aparche*) (1 Cor. 15:20, 23) that bodies will rise and that, because Jesus was resurrected, resurrections—and insurrections—are possible. This is the manifest side of the resurrection: the belief that God created and continues to create out of nothing, out of the experience of utter negativity. The resurrection is a demonstration of God's power that empowers. This moment isolated in itself, however, leads to what Douglas John Hall called "resurrectionism," the tendency to forget where we have come from and live in an aura of a pretense of optimism that is in denial about the challenges of this eon.

Paul detected this tendency in the community of Corinth, but the passage that best illustrates this attitude is the appearance of Jesus to the disciples hiding in the upper room (John 20:19-23). The story is known. Jesus suddenly comes into the room where the door was closed, where the disciples were closed in for fear of the people outside. And Jesus addresses them: "Peace be with you." All rejoice. But next comes a strange repetition when Jesus says once more: "Peace be with you." Jesus was a rabbi, a teacher, and an old saying reminds us that repetition is the mother of learning—*repetitio mater estudiorum est*. The disciples definitely did not get it the first time, so Jesus repeats it and then rephrases it in a third attempt to make himself understood: "As the Father has sent me, even so I send

---

[13] Morrison, *Beloved*, 217.
[14] Ibid., 135–36.

you." In other words, peace means "get out of here and do not be afraid." Peace is not a jolly party with the resurrected one, hidden in a closed room from a world that manufactures crosses.

"Sethe," he says, "me and you, we got more yesterday than anybody. We need some kind of tomorrow."[15]

The Resurrection Concealed

"Maybe I should leave things the way they are," she said. "How are they?" "We get along." "What about inside?" "I don't go inside."[16]

The manifest side of the resurrection can carry us out of that room. Empowerment is not an end in itself; it needs to carry us out into the world of danger and crosses. It reminds us of the fact that even if the body is raised the scars that testify to dangers are still there; they have not been erased. This is the moment to take the risk of being vulnerable in utter trust and faith. Paraphrasing Audre Lorde, we could say: because we have experienced healing and empowerment, we can face the world once more. Or in her words: "And true, experiencing old pain sometimes feels like hurling myself full force against a concrete wall. But I remind myself that I HAVE LIVED THROUGH IT ALL ALREADY, AND SURVIVED."[17]

Being enthralled at this station, however, leads to what can properly be called "cynicism." The disciples on the Emmaus road exemplify this attitude (Luke 24). All was over, and they hit the road to move forward. Crosses abound. That is the way it is in the world. No matter how much we try, the cycle of suffering will just go on. Let's leave Jerusalem. Life must go on. This station needs to lead us once more back to the manifest side of the cross; it is necessary to return to the site of the vile crime and

---

[15] Ibid., 273.

[16] Ibid., 45–46.

[17] Audre Lorde, *Sister Outsider: Essays and Speeches* (Freedom, Calif.: Crossing, 1984), 172; emphasis by the author.

be touched by the broken body once more, to be moved by the power of the cross and witness in that wretched tortured body the truth that in all the suffering of the world we meet the God with us, the God that dared to be emptied in solidarity with the human condition. Cynicism, however, holds us back.

> So they forgot her. Like an unpleasant dream during a troubling sleep. Occasionally, however, the rustle of a skirt hushes when they wake, and knuckles brushing a cheek in sleep seem to belong to the sleeper.[18]

A Diagram

In an attempt to represent graphically these "stations," I offer the following diagram: four stations are identified, each corresponding to a different place we stand in relation to the cross. Each moving arrow indicates how to move on and not be enthralled by a station, where the outward-moving arrows designate four problems surrounding theology of the cross: dolorism, defeatism, resurrectionism, and cynicism. The inward-pointed arrows describe the experience we need to own (suffering, void, empowerment, and scars). The vertical arrows indicate movements that entail love and mourning, truth and vulnerability. Finally, the crossing arrows indicate the movement from hope to transformation and witness to exposure. The whole diagram is flanked by the cross and resurrection, which frame its outer limits, suggesting a paradigm to frame our own existence between love and truth speaking (*parrhesia* or *satyagraha*).

---

[18] Morrison, *Beloved*, 275.

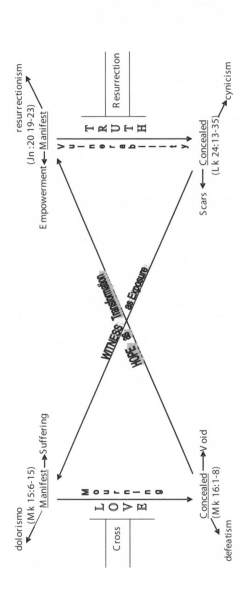

VIA CRUCIS ET RESURRECTIONIS
(Stations between the Cross and Resurrection)

Diagrams help us visualize ideas, but their help is like medicine; it is good when needed, but only when needed and within the prescribed doses, otherwise it is poison. The diagram should also carry a warning label as we find on medicine bottles: "Use as prescribed and keep out of reach of children." The worst shortcoming in this diagram that tries to convey the relationship between cross and resurrection is the horizontal shape suggesting a movement resembling the symbol for eternity. The diagram fails to account for the possibility that, at any of the points on the itinerary it describes, an end might just seize the moment, one that cannot be conveyed in the flat surface of its representation. And this end, the limit of the picture cannot be reproduced in the picture itself, for this might be how it all ends.

Coda

Consider the apocalypse of Jesus Christ, that empty time between Good Friday and Easter Sunday: an empty time in which nothing really happened; a time not to be filled for it was an apocalyptic time. And likewise consider the empty spaces: Golgotha, the place of hollow skulls where God dies, and the tomb which would be found to be empty. Indeed, apocalypses are dreadfully hollow. All the rest is quietness and immobility, no rush in the air, no *ruach*, no breath, no spirit stirring the face of the earth—or so we are led to believe.

Indeed, there is no third option to fill that time, to explain the meaning and connection between those hours that span Friday to Sunday. No words, as far as we know, are spoken there to accommodate, to negotiate the transaction between the *tremendum* and the *fascinans*. It was a moment of do-nothing (*otium*), the negation of negotiation (*nec-otium*).

But there is fragrance in the air, a scent of spices and perfume purchased by the women who have *seen* where the body of the Beloved One was laid (Mark 16:1). And there is a home where they went to prepare those spices and oils to anoint a decaying body (Luke 24:56). They have been spared, and on the Shabbat all was still—even in the midst of apocalypse. No words, instead a labor of mourning and love connects Friday and Sunday and fills the spaces of death with fragrance. The wind, the breath, the Spirit did not utter words on that day but spread a scent countering the miserable odor of death. There was work to be done even, and above all, in the midst of the apocalypse, a work of another economy, a mad economy (call it "grace-side economics") that spends for a gift that cannot be returned: spices for a dead and decaying body.

Those women, who have been spared in the midst of the apocalypse, saw salvation and new creation *first* because they gazed at the place where the Beloved died and the place where the body was laid. If it were not for those women, Christianity might possibly confess only to apparitions of Jesus—not to the resurrection of the body. What brings them with oil and spices to the tomb on Sunday is what Wendell Berry called the "practice of resurrection," a labor of mourning and love. It is also done because there was a place called home in the midst of the apocalypse. The time is not empty for there is an itinerary, a movement through spaces with a very clear trajectory. The movement goes from the limit, from the end (Good Friday, the cross, the tomb), to a center (the home, the Shabbat), and then back to the margin (Sunday, Easter, the tomb revisited).

We must realize that it is because of this movement, this liturgy, this labor of love and grieving, this graceful but mournful dance that we come to know that there is salvation, that there is new creation that springs exactly then, when the world ends—or there, where worlds end. Shall we dance?

Index